"A beautifully crafted tale of one man's grief – and a testament to the healing power of art. By inter-weaving the threads of his raw experience with strands of story, poetry, prose and photographs, Geoff Mead transforms his cruel and untimely loss into a tapestry of artful work and shining moments. There's a deep learning here and a visibly growing soul. Essential reading for those on the lonely road of bereavement."

– *William Ayot, poet and author of* Re-enchanting the Forest: Meaningful Ritual in a Secular Age

"A compelling read, reminding us of the importance of facing into grief, of finding creative ways to consciously mourn, thus finding solace for ourselves as well as honouring our loved one. I will be sharing this book widely as a handbook for conscious mourning that reminds us of the sweetness of life."

– *Juliet Grayson, Psychotherapist and author of* Landscapes of the Heart: The Working World of a Sex and Relationship Therapist

"A heartbreakingly moving and yet wonderfully hopeful chronicle of a unique and mysterious journey – from the shattering illness and death of his wife Chris to a beautiful reborn wholeness. Geoff unfolds the map of his grief over several years, from the first illness to the beginning of a new life and love. He offers no advice but this tale would be inspiring for anyone who has known loss of this depth. This is a story worthy of a great love, deeply borne."

– *Judith Hemming, Psychotherapist*

"A poignant and beautifully written account of life, love and grief. A personal story that will no doubt resonate with others who have lived through the death of someone they love."

– *Diana Crossley, Clinical Psychologist*

"Like a master poet, Geoff moves in and out of story and reality in this marvellous book. He invites us to walk alongside him as he shares his experience of loss, love and the birth of a new narrative."

– *David Drake, author of* Narrative Coaching:
Bringing Our New Stories to Life

"It is a privilege to bear witness to one man's deeply personal journey through the rocky terrain of grief, loss and bereavement, told with the raw pain and profound honesty of one who has been through the whirlwind and stepped out the other side. This will be a precious gift for others searching for comfort and solace whilst experiencing the anguish of losing a loved one."

– *Jaki Harris, Grief and Loss Specialist*

"*Gone in the Morning* is a testament to the power of writing to affirm, inquire and express doubt during difficult passages of life. Unswerving in its account, the reader is led alongside Geoff (and his charismatic Cockapoo, Ted) as he travels through 'active mourning'. His journey and his writing habits are an act to follow for the bereaved in this modest account of a recovery 'through' (not over) loss."

– *Claire Williamson, Programme Leader, MSc in Creative Writing for Therapeutic Purposes, Metanoia Institute*

"I am moved and inspired by Geoff's beautifully written and closely observed account of bereavement after his vivacious and extraordinarily creative wife Chris Seeley was diagnosed with a brain tumour and died 18 months later. It is a tribute to the therapeutic power of writing and above all a story of love, tenderness and hope. As someone recently bereaved myself, I found *Gone in the Morning* has invited me more fully into life, love and creativity."

– *Dr Julia Wallond, General Practitioner*

"As someone who has experienced the death of a spouse through illness, I recognise the archetypal journey through the landscape of bereavement that Geoff explores; as a storyteller working primarily with coaching people in the telling of their true life stories, I know that creating a coherent narrative from seemingly inexplicable life events brings understanding, acceptance and, ultimately, peace. When that story is told well, those benefits spread. This is such a story."

– *Sue Hollingsworth, Centre for Biographical Storytelling*

"Written with immediacy and resonance, poignancy and humour, *Gone in the Morning* strikes a fine balance between life and loss. Geoff Mead's warmly human writing voice makes it a trusty companion in this most solitary of human experiences. I am grateful that this book has been written."

– *Barbara Turner-Vesselago, author of* Writing Without a Parachute: The Art of Freefall

"Geoff's quiet, unassuming writing celebrates his late wife's creativity and explores his own challenges in being alone without his soulmate. The perceptive bereavement worker will find much of use and the bereaved themselves can draw on the rawness of emotion and the growth of hope as he works through his first two years of widowhood."

– *Janet Dowling, Bereavement Counsellor*

by the same author

Coming Home to Story
Storytelling Beyond Happily Ever After
ISBN 978 1 90836 301 5
eISBN 978 1 78450 455 7

of related interest

A Matter of Life and Death
60 Voices Share their Wisdom
Rosalind Bradley
Foreword by Archbishop Emeritus Desmond Tutu
ISBN 978 1 84905 601 4
eISBN 978 1 78450 283 6

If You Sit Very Still
Marian Partington
Foreword by Marina Cantacuzino
ISBN 978 1 78592 140 7
eISBN 978 1 78450 407 6

Writing My Way Through Cancer
Myra Schneider
ISBN 978 1 84310 113 0
eISBN 978 1 84642 400 7

GONE IN THE MORNING

A WRITER'S JOURNEY OF BEREAVEMENT

GEOFF MEAD

Jessica Kingsley *Publishers*
London and Philadelphia

The image on page 13, "Maelstrom, Carta Marina," by Berig is reproduced from Wikimedia Commons in accordance with the Creative Commons Attribution-Share Alike 3.0 License (https://commons.wikimedia.org/wiki/File%3AMaelstrom%2C_Carta_Marina. png). The image on page 21, "Night Jetty," is reproduced with kind permission from Martin Bailey. The poem "Out Beyond Ideas" by Rumi on page 47 is reproduced with kind permission of its translator Coleman Barks. The image on page 50, "Tomba Celle (Cimitero di Staglieno)" by Giulio Monteverde, is reproduced from Wikimedia Commons in accordance with the Creative Commons Attribution-Share Alike 3.0 License (https://commons.wikimedia.org/wiki/File%3ATomba_Celle_(Cimitero_ di_Staglieno)%2C_opera_di_Giulio_Monteverde%2C_1893.jpg). The image on page 81, *Ulysses and Penelope* by Francesco Primaticcio, is reproduced from Wikimedia Commons with kind permission of The Yorck Project (https://commons.wikimedia. org/wiki/File:Francesco_Primaticcio_002.jpg). The image on page 132, "Wild Woman Artist," is reproduced with kind permission from Kathy Mead Skerritt. The image on page 161, "Numitorium," is reproduced with kind permission from Paul Macdonald.

First published in 2018
by Jessica Kingsley Publishers
73 Collier Street
London N1 9BE, UK
and
400 Market Street, Suite 400
Philadelphia, PA 19106, USA

www.jkp.com

Copyright © Geoff Mead 2018

Library of Congress Cataloging in Publication Data
A CIP catalog record for this book is available from the Library of Congress

British Library Cataloguing in Publication Data
A CIP catalogue record for this book is available from the British Library

ISBN 978 1 78592 355 5
eISBN 978 1 78450 691 9

Printed and bound in Great Britain

CHRIS SEELEY
21 August 1966–3 December 2014

Machete
hacking at the mooring lines
tying me to my life, the
shore, the jetty of my life
as the tide comes in and
oh so gradually
bits disappear
under the starlight
and others float off to sea.
Gone in the morning.

From the journal of Chris Seeley,
23 November 2014

PREFACE

Recently, a friend gave me a copy of Joan Didion's *The Year of Magical Thinking* tied with a gold ribbon. I'd misplaced my old copy so I was pleased to have a new one. I untied the ribbon and looked for a half-remembered passage that had struck me as important when I'd first read it. I recalled that Didion had written about a moment of realisation about six months after the death of her husband John Gregory Dunne. Ah yes. There it was on page 147: "Until now I had been able only to grieve, not mourn. Grief was passive. Mourning, the act of dealing with grief, required attention."

Yes, I thought. Grief has a mind of its own; it comes in waves, often when you least expect it. The smallest thing catches at your heartstrings and you are undone. We cannot choose its form or timing. All we can do is deal with it – and that requires us to pay exquisite attention to memories, feelings and intuitions. Mourning is a conscious process to which we can bring our creativity, passion and intelligence. In doing so, we both honour those we have lost and comfort ourselves. And isn't that what the departed want for us: to live well and be happy? Isn't that what we would wish on our death beds for the loved ones we are leaving behind?

I'm a writer, so when my wife died from the effects of a brain tumour, I sought solace in the exercise of my craft. Writing became my way of mourning her loss. This book is an account of my experience of the *terra incognita* of grief, based on what I wrote at the time. I hope that there is something of value in it for all who have grieved because, if we open our hearts, we may be able to recognise something of each other and feel less alone in our suffering. We may even glimpse the possibility of joy hiding in the shadows.

CONTENTS

CHAPTER 1

HERE BE DRAGONS

Every grief is both universal and unique. Every journey of bereavement takes us into uncharted territory. My journey began in August 2013, when my wife Chris Seeley was diagnosed with an inoperable brain tumour. She died, only 48 years old, in December 2014.

It wasn't meant to happen that way.

We met when I was 51 and she was 34. I was divorced with four grown-up children and Chris had never been married. She had also, she told me, "chosen to be child-free." We came together through a mutual love of storytelling and as action-researchers studying in the same institution; I was just finishing my doctorate as she was starting hers. For 12 years we lived interdependently, sometimes under the same roof and sometimes apart.

There was nothing she wasn't interested in and little she couldn't do well. She lived artfully, bringing her creative talent and prodigious energy to everything she did, whether it was painting, teaching, clowning or making friends. Supporting each other's creativity was at the heart of our relationship. She encouraged me to write, helped me get published, and wept with joy when I told her a few weeks before she died that I would dedicate myself to being a writer.

That Chris (talented, exuberant and gregarious) chose to love introverted, melancholic me is one of life's great mysteries. But love me she did, and I loved her too, though it wasn't until she became seriously ill that I fully appreciated how profound and rare a love we had.

Our lives changed in a moment, on 24 August 2013, while on holiday in Portugal, when she had a massive seizure. Within a few days, she was diagnosed with a brain tumour, inoperable because it was too deep for surgeons to reach without causing catastrophic injury. Our first decision on hearing the diagnosis was to get married. From the beginning we decided to face her illness and death together. She was determined to live as fully as possible until the very end and I committed myself to supporting her.

She was given medication to reduce the likelihood of further seizures and we returned home. We didn't know how long she had to live but the clock was ticking. It turned out to be 12 months before her seizures returned. We got married, bought a camper van, and acquired a Cockapoo puppy called Ted. Chris wasn't allowed to drive so I became her chauffeur. We lived in Folly Cottage, her tiny house in the Cotswolds, did a little bit of work, spent time with friends, and did everything together.

As the tumours grew and multiplied in Chris's brain, they affected first her mobility and later her cognition. After several stays in hospital, she came home where I cared for her, with the support of friends and some professional help, until she died on 3 December 2014, just ten days before our first wedding anniversary.

It was a good year, in some ways the best we had together, our appreciation of each other heightened by the knowledge that it would not last. It's hard to be with someone you love when they are dying. But it is also a privilege: an opportunity to say and do what is needed to prepare for the moment of separation; a chance to resolve matters and find peace in each other's arms; a lesson in the harsh beauty of love.

રે રે.રે રે

A few weeks after Chris's death, a wise friend emailed to ask me if – as a storyteller – I knew a particular story that might sustain me in my grief. I hadn't asked myself that question and I didn't have an immediate answer for him. However, over the next few days, one story tapped me on the shoulder and wouldn't go away. It was the old Scandinavian tale of *The Lindworm* that I'd known for years and occasionally performed. Without thinking too much, I sat down and wrote out a version such as I might tell. I wasn't concerned with how the story began so much as how it ended and so I came in halfway through.

> The king and queen of that land tried one last time to find a bride for their eldest son, but as he was half-human and half-dragon, and had already demolished several prospective partners, no more princesses were willing to take the risk.
>
> But a shepherd's daughter saw the royal proclamation. She'd caught sight of the royal heir once when visiting the city. Those around her called him "the Lindworm" under their breath. He didn't seem very scary to her; a bit stuck-up perhaps; a bit self-centred. But maybe, she thought, there was someone worthy of love under all that scaly armour. She decided that she would offer her hand in marriage and set off for the palace.
>
> On the way, she met an old woman who asked her where she was going.
>
> "I'm going to the palace to marry the Lindworm," she replied.
>
> "You've heard about the disappearing princesses?"
>
> "Oh yes."
>
> "I hope you are well-prepared. Do you have your wedding shift?"
>
> "I do."
>
> "You'll need more than one," said the old woman, looking into her eyes.
>
> "I have seven," the shepherd's daughter said. "I embroidered them myself."

"That's good," said the old woman. "I expect princesses get other people to embroider theirs. Be sure to wear them all."

"All of them?"

"Yes. All seven," said the old woman, turning to go. "Good luck."

A shepherd's daughter wasn't quite what they'd had in mind, but in the absence of another princess, the king and queen accepted her offer. She was fresh-faced and lovely. She seemed intelligent too, despite her desire to marry their son.

In those days, the bride and groom enjoyed their nuptials the night before the wedding ceremony. So, that evening – with fanfares and flourishes – the king and queen led the chosen one to their son's chamber, let her in and closed the door behind her.

She stood upright and fearless in her wedding clothes as her intended husband emerged from behind a tapestry. Tall, his skin polished like scaly armour, he stared admiringly at her slender form.

"Strip," he said, moving towards her.

She looked straight back at him. "I'll take off one of my shifts if you take off one of your skins," she said.

The Lindworm stopped in his tracks. "No-one has ever asked me to do that before," he said. His gaze softened a little from desire to longing as he grasped a skin and pulled it off over his head, grunting with pain. The shepherd's daughter removed an embroidered shift and dropped it to the floor.

"Strip," said the Lindworm.

"I'll take off another of my shifts if you take off another of your skins," she replied.

The Lindworm tore off a second layer of polished scaly armour and the shepherd's daughter dropped a second shift.

"Again," said the Lindworm.

And so they repeated the process again and again until, crying out in agony, the Lindworm stripped off the last of his seven skins and the shepherd's daughter stood naked before him. Now he was utterly flayed, a pulsating mass of red flesh. The shepherd's daughter called for a bucket of lye and a scrubbing brush and she scrubbed the Lindworm until the bristles were worn out and he was quite raw.

When she was done, she called for a bucket of milk with which she bathed the Lindworm's trembling body. Then she took him to bed and held him tenderly in her arms until they both fell asleep.

The next morning, when the palace servants brought breakfast to the happy couple, they were sitting up in bed smiling: a prince of the realm – no longer a dragon – and his true bride.

The more I thought about what I had written, the more I could see the parallels between the story and the commitment that Chris and I had made to face her illness and death together. As with us, it was the couple's willingness to strip off layer after layer until each was, in their own way, naked and defenceless that enabled them to achieve (if only momentarily) a sense of complete mutual acceptance and union. We too had been flayed and stripped bare by successive events until, as Chris moved towards death, nothing stood between us. Our final conversation bathed my soul in a way that will nourish me for the rest of my days.

Then death picked up the brush and began to scrub.

I was moved to start writing again. I realised that I had to write about Chris's death and the life we shared during her illness. I wrote in bursts, over several weeks; I wrote through tears and rage; through love and laughter; through anguish and despair, until I was spent and it was done.

I followed the form of the story, writing the memoir in seven acts, corresponding to the seven skins and seven shifts shed by the Lindworm and the shepherd's daughter, marking the stages of our final journey towards love and intimacy.

I wrote about Chris's first seizure in Portugal; our wedding; the day of the biopsy; treatment in hospital; palliative care at home; her final few days; and how she died. I wrote to relive rather than to explain or analyse what happened. It's as honest and unadorned an account as I could manage. Some of it features in this book.

Completing those stories helped me to appreciate the solace that writing can bring. Now they're down on paper, I don't have to cling to the memories quite so tightly and they don't weigh me down as much. But the process of writing is just as important to me as what I write. The struggle to express my experience of bereavement in words is a kind of offering to Chris's memory.

I also wrote regular blog posts. Memories, acts of remembrance, and the everyday events of life triggered the impulse to write more publicly. I chronicled my responses to Chris's passing, the twists and turns of grief, and the ways in which I have sought to mourn her loss. Sometimes, I've written a poem to explore a particularly powerful moment or feeling. Crafting a poem seems to offer me a deeper, more sustained form of enquiry than writing prose.

All this writing has served me well. None of it has diminished the pain of losing Chris. Rather it has heightened my experience of grief and deepened my understanding of how conscious mourning keeps things moving. I have gone through the whole gamut of emotions, but I've never felt stuck. Piece by piece, I have negotiated the narrative wreckage of Chris's death and begun to re-story my life.

৯ ৯ ৯ ৯

Recently, I was having a beer with a friend. He asked me what I was writing these days and I told him that I'd written a memoir about the last 18 months of Chris's life, about 150 blogs and a bunch of poems, mostly about grief. He gave me a quizzical look and asked a pointed question: "You are getting over this thing, aren't you?"

"I'm not trying to get over it," I replied. "I'm trying to get through it."

He took in my reply but said nothing.

"Writing seems to help," I added.

"Really?" he said, and changed the subject.

It was a fair challenge, and not meant unkindly. I've been thinking about it, off and on, ever since. Why had I been so adamant about not wanting to get over Chris's death? What had I meant when I said that I was trying to get through it?

The other day I woke up with a realisation so blindingly obvious that it had hitherto escaped me. "Getting over it" was reminiscent of how my mother attempted to help me deal with my father's death when I was a little boy. She loved him dearly and I know from conversations much later in life that she was heartbroken when he died. But she dealt with the situation by resolutely refusing to look back. Whatever she was feeling herself, she acted in public as though Dad had never existed. I was not taken to his funeral and cannot recall him ever being spoken of in my presence. She remarried six years later and the few remaining photographs of my father disappeared from the walls. With the very best of intentions, she had denied me the chance to mourn his loss.

Consequently, it took me half a lifetime, some very challenging conversations, and many years of therapy to "get over" his death.

In the end we managed to rehabilitate him into our lives and I had the wonderful privilege when my mother died of interring her ashes in his grave, as she had requested.

So, I have no intention of trying to "get over" Chris's death. Instead, I try to "get through" my grief and sense of loss by performing conscious acts of mourning. I take whatever time I need to say goodbye: at her funeral and later at the celebration of her life; by caring for her memorial stone; on my peregrination around the world with her ashes; and through my writing of memoir, stories, poetry and blogs.

This is my way of trying to navigate the *terra incognita* of grief. I am as lost and as determined to come through as my mother was. Nothing can prepare you for such a loss and no-one else can tell you how to survive it.

Elizabeth Kübler-Ross described the landscape of loss in terms we can all understand: shock – denial – anger – bargaining – depression – acceptance. It is useful for anyone who has been bereaved to know this generalised pattern of reaction. It helps us to normalise the emotional roller-coaster that follows the death of a loved one and to understand that grief has many faces.

Despite this knowledge, we are strangers in a strange land, seeking our own unique ways to bear our sorrows. The ancient cartographers knew a thing or two: once we enter this unknown territory there are raging dragons waiting to pounce and fathomless whirlpools eager to drown us in depression.

> The map of grief is dark and difficult to read.
> Whole continents shift; islands disappear.
> Nothing is where it's supposed to be.
>
> *Hic sunt dracones* warn the old cartographers.
> Fiery-breathed dragons weeping tears of blood,
> Hungry for those who speak the language of the dead.
>
> *Hic est horrenda caribdis* they admonish,
> A whirlpool made of sorrow and of pain,
> Ready to engulf us in self-pity.
>
> And if these terrors should be sleeping when we pass,
> There lurk the hidden reefs of memory
> To breach our hulls below the waterline.

There are a thousand ways to founder in the deep.
The wreckage of the grieving and bereaved
Is strewn beneath the billow of the waves.

For those of us who navigate these dismal shores
There's no known passage and no guarantee
That we will make it through the stricken sea.

As a writer, I try to make sense of the world through the process of writing. I have published several books, including a volume of poetry, but most of what I've written since Chris died is simply what I needed to write for myself to soothe my grief. Some people keep journals, but I'm a sloppy journal-keeper. I need the presence of potential readers to exercise my craft and to keep me going. So, even though I wrote for my own reasons, I have posted some of this writing online. To my surprise, I received many comments from readers encouraging me to share the account of my journey more widely because they found it moving and helpful to read when confronting their own losses and disappointments.

At the time of putting pen to paper, 18 months have passed since Chris died. I am writing from within the shifting experience of grief. Shifting not in a neat linear progression from one phase to the next, but shifting nonetheless, because nothing in life stands still. The dragons and the whirlpools, the reefs and lurking horrors of the deep, catch me from time to time. But, as I am beginning to discover, there are also islands of happiness; an ocean of beautiful memories; and always the prospect of love and new life on the horizon.

I have learned much and continue to learn: I am not where I was in my life 18 months ago and, in some sense, I am not *who* I was then either. Bereavement shatters our identity; I knew who I was when Chris was alive but I'm having to rediscover myself in her absence. Of one thing, I am sure: only to the extent that I embrace my sorrow do I also open myself to life and love and joy.

વ વ વ વ

This book is the story of a bereavement. Like all real life stories, it is made from the shards of shattered dreams, glued together by hope and happenstance.

It begins with an ending.

CHAPTER 2

GONE IN THE MORNING

Dr Guglani, the consultant oncologist, sat on the end of Chris's bed.

"The treatment is doing you more harm than good," he said. "If it's quality of life you are after, we should stop now."

His words were shocking but they did not come as a surprise to either of us. The decline in her condition had been rapid. Within ten days, she had gone from swimming with me every evening at Calcot Spa to being unable to stand. I knew that she wanted to die gracefully rather than cling on to the last vestiges of life. We asked a couple of questions, including the one we really didn't want to ask. His answer was diplomatic and compassionate: "All I can say is that I think it will be shorter rather than longer."

He means weeks not months, I thought to myself. Fuck. **Fuck. FUCK.** I bit my lip and squeezed Chris's hand.

"OK," she said. "Stop the treatment. When can I go home?"

It took a while to get the house ready for her while she worked with the occupational therapists and had some intensive physiotherapy to help her get around with walkers and a wheelchair. She finally made it back home to Folly Cottage on Monday 13 October 2014. We didn't know it then, of course, but we were to have only another seven weeks together.

☙ ☙ ☙ ☙

It happened quickly in the end.

On Monday 1 December, after visiting us for Thanksgiving, our friends Dick and Karen leave for New York. As they go, another friend, Sue Hollingsworth, arrives to lend a hand for a few days. The next morning, Chris is too weak to get out of bed, even with the help of Liz and Kate, the agency staff. By mid-morning, she has fallen into a deep sleep and by the afternoon it's clear that she is unconscious.

Her breathing gets harsher and more rasping as her body fights to keep her alive. The district nurse delivers morphine and a syringe driver, checks Chris over and helps Sue and me get her into a nightdress, change the bedding, and put her in a stable position on her left side.

"She can hear you," says the nurse. "She knows you are here."

"That's good to know. We'll stay with her," I say.

I telephone Joan and Helen (Chris's mum and sister) and suggest that they come to see her. Helen says she'll come this evening and Joan makes plans to travel the next morning. During the afternoon, Sue and I take it in turns to sit by Chris's side and talk to her. Ted lies next to her on the bed, tail between his legs, and snuffles plaintively. He is sensitive to every mood and I imagine that they are communing somehow.

Helen arrives at about 7.00pm with her partner Sam and daughter Rosie. We manage to eat something while making sure there is always someone in the room with Chris. She doesn't move or respond to our presence but she's still breathing strongly. Just after 9.30pm I compose an email and send it to as many of our friends as I can reach.

Please light a candle or say a prayer for Chris who became very poorly over the weekend. She has been unconscious all day today although sometimes she seems to be aware of what is going on around her. She is surrounded by love: mine, Ted's, her sister Helen's, and our friend Sue Hollingsworth who is staying for a few days. Widening circles of love hold her in their embrace: you, her many other friends, her former students, colleagues, the doctors, nurses, and carers whose hearts she has touched. Her warm and generous soul is beginning its journey home.

Love, light and blessings to you all, our soul buddies.

Geoff & Chris xx

The word spreads. Messages of love and support flood in and later I learn that scores of candles were lit for Chris that night in more than a dozen countries around the world.

At about 11.00pm we tuck her up for the night and make our way to bed. Helen and Sam sleep upstairs; Rosie is in the camper van; Sue stays in the kitchen just a few yards away from Chris; she promises to call me if anything happens and I go out into the Shepherd Hut in the garden with Ted. I fall into bed, exhausted, and close my eyes.

I wake at about 4.00am and cannot get back to sleep. I light a candle, crawl out of bed and pull on my cold clothes. I pee in the garden, then go quietly back into the sitting room where Chris is lying in bed. She is exactly where we left her and still breathing hard. I kiss her face and sit down in an armchair in the corner of the room. Ted sits at my feet as I open my laptop and work at a poem that I know Chris will never see. I have no idea why, but what comes up is the image of her sitting at the kitchen table painstakingly applying eyeliner. She's never used makeup before, but she bought a selection of eyeliners and mascara when she got home from hospital and started using them. She calls them her "eye-pokers."

I wonder what moved you,
who never wore makeup,
to take up eyeliner and mascara.

"Poking at my eyes"
you called it, as you perched
for an hour or more,

smiling into the mirror,
like a girl getting ready
for Saturday night out.

I was secretly flattered,
thinking that it was me
you wanted to please.

Only now it dawns on me
that you want to *shine*
for your date with death.

The house wakes up slowly. We drink tea and make toast for breakfast. Liz and Kate turn up from Prestige Home+Care at 9.45am. They change Chris's nightclothes and replace the sheets. "She's got some bedsores," Liz says. "You'd better have a look." We find two small abrasions and I call the district nurse to let her know. She promises to call round soon to dress the sores. "It's alright," she says. "She can't feel them."

Dr Thompson, our GP, arrives at 11.00am and examines her. "How long?" I ask when we are out of earshot.

"A few days, perhaps. We can't be certain."

"Her breathing sounds more laboured," I say. "It's rasping and rattling."

"That's just the usual secretions. She's not swallowing now. The district nurse can give her an injection when she comes to dry them up a bit. That will help her breathe more easily."

The doctor goes. The district nurse calls in to do her stuff. Joan arrives late morning. Sue, Helen, Sam and Rosie all want to spend time with Chris. Sarah and Carole both visit. I remember something that Chris asked me to arrange and I spend an hour trying to sort it out upstairs on the computer. The house has turned into Piccadilly Circus. My rational self knows that it's important for people to see Chris before she dies but it feels like they are taking her away from me. Just when I most want her to myself, she has become public property. When William and Juliet (who officiated at our wedding) phone to ask if they can visit in the evening, I almost say, "No."

They arrive at about 6.30pm as Sue is in the kitchen with Sam and Rosie, getting supper organised. Helen and Joan are with Chris.

"Hello, lovely boy," says William as he enters, in a jokey Welsh accent. His large comforting presence undoes me; I fall into his outstretched arms and cry my heart out.

Joan and Helen make way for Juliet who holds Chris's hand in hers and speaks softly to her. William leads me into the bedroom but I still can't hear what Juliet is saying.

After a few minutes, Juliet raises her voice: "I just need to tell you that Chris hasn't breathed for a while." I break free of William's embrace and go over to the bed. Chris's face, which had been red with the effort of breathing, is returning to normal. "Chris," I call out. "Chris." I hold her. Her body has relaxed. She is soft and warm.

I can hear several voices singing an advent carol in the kitchen: "O Come, O Come, Emmanuel." It's an unusual sound for this house but it feels comforting and appropriate. Juliet leaves the room and returns with a mirror. She holds it in front of Chris's face to check for condensation. Nothing. "She's gone," she says. "What's the time?"

"6.47," says someone.

I feel winded, as though I've been mule-kicked. I hold on to her, as if this will somehow stem the flow of time. But 6.48 arrives, then 6.49 and I can do nothing to stop the clock. Eventually, William takes me into the kitchen and sits me down. He pours me a large whisky and I drink the spirit neat. It burns my throat, warms my stomach, and – for a few moments – quells the ache in my heart.

Someone calls the out-of-hours number for the surgery and a duty doctor is summoned to pronounce Chris dead and take details for the death certificate. I decide that I want to sit in vigil all night. William and Juliet cannot stay and Chris's family say they would rather not. Joan returns to her hotel two hundred yards up the road; Helen and Sam go to the Shepherd Hut to sleep, and Rosie hunkers down in the camper van for a second night.

"Who do you want?" asks Sue.

"Just a few people who were around near the end: you, Carole, Sarah."

"You should have a man as well. Who can you call?"

"Peter Neall, I suppose, but it's getting late."

"Call him if you want him. He can decide for himself."

I call Carole and Sarah first. Carole says she'll come in an hour. Sarah feels too exhausted to travel. Peter says, "Yes," immediately, arrives two hours later and stays for four days.

We gather round the bed; drink tea and whisky; talk about old times; relive the glories of our wedding (they were all guests); weep and laugh; meditate and sing; eat sandwiches; doze when we can't keep our eyes open; sit on the bed and cuddle Chris; comfort Ted who is very puzzled by this latest turn of events; and consider ourselves blessed to be here together at this time.

The night passes. Another dawn comes. Chris looks peaceful. I hope she is pleased with how we have been and what we have done. I remember that I had seen her writing something that looked like poetry in the margins of her journal when we were at the Medicine Unboxed conference just ten days before. I leaf through its pages and find these words:

> Machete
> hacking at the mooring lines
> tying me to my life, the
> shore, the jetty of my life
> as the tide comes in and
> oh so gradually
> bits disappear
> under the starlight
> and others float off to sea.
> Gone in the morning.

She'd always said that she was "a bit crap" at poetry. But here was proof of the contrary. Her words deserve to be seen, I decide, and I include them in the email that I send out to tell people that she has died.

Joan, Helen, Sam and Rosie appear for breakfast. They spend a few minutes with Chris and then leave to go home. Sue says goodbye and leaves me with Peter. He calls the undertaker at my request and Jeremy Clutterbuck arrives at noon.

As soon as he arrives, I know that I'm not ready for Chris to leave the house. I want her to myself for one more day. "No problem," says Jeremy. "You decide when you're ready. It's entirely up to you."

We talk a little about funeral arrangements. "Actually, Chris said, 'Stick me in a cardboard box and chuck me on a bonfire,'" I tell him.

"We do have a cardboard coffin, although it's not our cheapest," he says.

I'm delighted and order one. We can write on that, I think to myself. Jeremy takes a few more details and then leaves.

I spend the afternoon with Chris. I read her the whole of *Bear Child*, a story that I wrote for her while she was in hospital; I sleep beside her on the bed for a while; she seems to listen while I tell her stories about our time together; I remind her how much I love her.

At about 7.00pm, Sarah, Tim and Julia arrive. Sarah had asked if I would like them to come and meditate and I welcomed the idea. We sit in silence in a circle around Chris for about 20 minutes, then Sarah leads us in the same mantra that she and Julia had chanted with Chris in hospital the night the consultant had told us that the treatment was not working.

> Gaté gaté pãragaté
> Pãrasam gaté
> Bodhi svãhã

We repeat it several times to close our meditation. Tim, Julia and Sarah say their goodbyes to Chris and we go into the kitchen to eat the soup that Sarah had brought with her. "What does the chant mean?" I ask her.

"It's Sanskrit and probably untranslatable," she says. "But it means something like: *Going, going, going beyond – going utterly beyond – oh what an awakening.*"

I look in on Chris on my way to bed. Something has changed: she was peaceful before but now she looks utterly tranquil. "Her soul is leaving us," I think. I sleep upstairs again while Peter bunks down in the kitchen to be on hand in case I should need anything. I shut the bedroom door, haul Ted onto the bed and sleep, undisturbed, for hours.

In the morning, I go downstairs. Overnight, Chris's face has become mottled and there are small frothy bubbles on her lips. I am looking at a corpse. I ask Peter to arrange for the undertakers to take the body away. We have breakfast and wait for their arrival. Before they come, there is a knock on the door. It's an old friend, Ashley Ramsden. "I just had to come," he says. He spends a quarter of an hour in the bedroom then takes me and Ted out for a walk in Kingscote Woods. When we get back, Chris's body has gone and the bed has been tidied up. "They did a good job," says Peter.

We pull something together for lunch before Ashley has to go and then Peter and I go out for the afternoon with Ted. We leave the window in the bedroom open a crack to help the air circulate, and drive into Cirencester to register Chris's death. I show the registrar our marriage certificate to prove that we were married. "That's my signature," she says. "You don't remember, but I was deputy registrar at Stroud when you got married. Did you know she was ill then?"

"Yes," I say. "But we were hoping for longer."

Ted lies at our feet for 30 minutes or so while the formalities are completed. Then we leave the building and go out into the fresh air. "How about a coffee and a visit to the shops?" I say. "It feels like I haven't been out of the house for weeks."

We have coffee and cake at the Cotswold Artisan Coffee Shop; I buy a pair of blue and red striped pyjamas from Pakeman, Catto and Carter because I fancy being extravagant. We look in a couple of shops for some dried sage that we can burn to purify the house, find nothing and drive to Stroud where we get two fine bundles of white sage at a stall in the indoor market.

It's dark by the time we get back to Folly Cottage. I unlock the front door, turn on the lights and step inside. I notice a fluttering movement out of the corner of my eye. Perched on my Panama hat on the kitchen windowsill is a robin. "How did it get in here?" I think, and then remember the window we had left slightly open. Ted stares intently at the bird but makes no sound. Peter follows me in to the house. "Look, a robin," I say. We gaze at it with a sense of wonder as it looks in our direction, hops into the air, flits round the kitchen twice and flies out of the open door into the night. "Wow," I say, tears in my eyes. "How wonderful."

A few days later, remembering Chris's poem and with the image of the robin still vivid in my mind, I write these verses:

Robin Redbreast,
welcome harbinger,
thorn-pricked
    at Calvary
        it's said.

Caught inside our kitchen,
waiting for an open door,
sweet songbird,
    holy creature,
        wild and free,

Unmoored,
untethered at last,
unconfined by earthly weight,
    your spirit soars
        into the night.

The night of the robin, I sleep soundly. My last waking thought is to vow that I will put out plenty of food in the garden to look after the birds during the winter months. The next day, we get up early, light the sage bundles and spend a couple of hours "smudging" every room in the house, wafting the aromatic fumes into every corner to drive out the acrid smell of death.

Afterwards, Peter leaves for home. I wave goodbye as he drives down the road then go back inside the house. I walk around the empty rooms, as though Chris might be there somewhere, waiting to tell me what to do now that she's gone. I make a cup of coffee and sit at the kitchen table, still piled high with the detritus of her final illness: boxes of pills; letters from the hospital; a pair of spectacles; her makeup bag containing her "eye-pokers"; the special fork with a cutting edge she bought because she could only use her right hand; emergency phone numbers; lists of appointments; books she never got to read.

"So this is it," I think. "I'm a widower."

Looking back now, I can see that the extraordinary gift of the robin's symbolic ascension provided a wonderful image of Chris returning to the cosmos. Towards the end of her life she was increasingly conscious of herself as star-stuff, composed (as we all are) of atoms forged in the hearts of exploding stars. In hospital she had written a note in the margin of her journal: "Welcome Home Stardust." It comforts me to know that she died with a sense of homecoming and I am very aware of her presence every time I look at the night sky.

I have no firm beliefs about death or what (if anything) happens afterwards. I simply have the experience of being close to Chris when she died. I used to think that the term "passing" was a euphemism used by those too squeamish to talk about dying. But I now understand that death is not instantaneous, it's a process that takes time. It took two days for Chris's unique essence to depart after she stopped breathing. Staying with her and witnessing her soul, her spirit, her life-force (or whatever we call it) leave her body was hugely important. It was my first conscious act of mourning and set the tone for everything that followed.

Very soon I would have to arrange her funeral.

CHAPTER 3

WILD MARGINS

The earliest I could book the crematorium was for Monday 15 December. They offered Friday 12 December but that was my birthday and I wanted to keep the cremation separate. I was also acutely aware that it would be our first anniversary on Saturday 13 December and it felt important to wait until after that, as if somehow it would mean that we had managed a full year of married life.

My daughter Georgie came up from London for my birthday. We watched an old movie together on the DVD player and the next morning scouted around for a pub or hotel in which to hold the wake after Chris's cremation. We found one a few miles from home, which had a proper fire and a bar we could take over.

Georgie left that afternoon and I drove over to Chepstow to spend the evening with William and Juliet. They cooked dinner for me – beef stew. Juliet made three times as much as we needed and put the remainder in Tupperware boxes for my freezer to make sure I wouldn't starve. They offered me a bed but Ted was getting restless so I drove home to Folly Cottage.

Home without Chris. It was a strange thought. The night sky was clear and full of stars. One year since we got married. We should have been celebrating our Paper Anniversary. Then I remembered that there was a box of Chinese lanterns in the house. I got one out and unfolded the tissue paper.

One match was enough to light the fuel cell. I held the lantern by the top as the flame heated the air inside the canopy, filling it out. I felt the lantern begin to pull against gravity but released it too soon. It snagged on the rowan tree in the back garden. I managed to shake it loose only to see it drift into next door's garden and get caught in a bush. I ran round to set it free.

By the time I got there, it had lifted itself into the air and was climbing fast. It just made it over the rooftops and rose higher and higher into the sky, soaring over the village and the surrounding fields and woods. I followed it with my eyes until it became a tiny pinprick of light sailing through the night towards the constellation of the Great Bear. She felt very close.

Then it was gone from my sight.

I went indoors. I decided it was time to sleep in Chris's bed. The linen had been changed, but otherwise it looked identical to the day she died. I put on my pyjamas, made a cup of tea and a hot water bottle, and lit a candle in front of the picture of Chris and me on our wedding day.

Three small bowls, one of salt, one of rice and one of water, were arrayed round the candle to speed Chris on her journey. They were Juliet's idea. I refreshed them each day and told Chris whatever was on my mind. Usually I just said what I'd been doing that day, but sometimes there was more. I couldn't predict what would come out. That night, I wished her a happy anniversary, blew out the candle and climbed into bed. Ted jumped up beside me where Chris would have been.

I pulled the covers up to my shoulders and lay in the dark, thinking about the funeral service that was going to happen the day after next. Chris and I had talked about what she wanted: "A quiet cremation; nothing fancy; just family and close friends. Ask them not to wear black, anything but black. And a bang-up party in a few months' time." She'd left the details to me and, after she died, I asked Peter if he would help me put together and conduct the service. His advice was invaluable: "We can do this however you want. You don't have to please anyone else. No shoulds and oughts. Do whatever you think is right for her and for you."

We'd talked about flowers and music and poetry and readings and who we would ask to do what. I guessed that I wouldn't feel up to speaking. Things seemed to fall into place easily. Peter drafted an order of service and sent it to me. It was perfect: simple, profound, authentic and creative. "You've thought of everything," I said.

But there was something else that no-one could help me with. The undertaker, Jeremy Clutterbuck, had rung me a few days before. "What would you like Chris to be wearing when she's cremated?" he'd asked.

His question took me by surprise. I hadn't given any previous thought to what she should wear, but I knew straight away that it had to be her wedding dress. In the face of her disastrous diagnosis, getting married had been the only thing that made sense. Our wedding had been magnificent, beautiful and eccentric. She had worn a flame-coloured silk dress made for her in Sri Lanka. It was still hanging in the wardrobe. I wanted to affirm my love for her: I wanted her to be cremated as my bride. In the last few weeks of her life, doctors, nurses, therapists, carers, friends and relatives had filled the house. She had become public property and I wanted to reclaim her for myself.

I took the dress to Clutterbuck's office in Dursley, along with a hat that she had worn in her last weeks to cover her radiation-damaged hair, a copy of a poem that I'd written for her, called "We Who Love You," and the teddy bear that I'd given her when we first got to know each other. "Would it be alright for her to have these with her when she is cremated?" I'd asked.

"Of course," they said. "We'll see to it."

I'd told no-one else what I'd done. I wanted it to be our secret: hers and mine. She would wear her wedding clothes and so would I. As her body was consumed by the fire, we would somehow re-forge our bond as husband and wife. We would always be married.

"I've done what I can," I thought, as I drifted towards sleep. "I hope you like it, sweetheart."

The next day was a blur. Karen arrived from New York; my older daughter Nicky flew in from Dubai and Georgie brought her from the airport. We talked, we ate, but I felt numb: waiting – my life suspended – for the funeral.

We got up early on Monday morning. It was cold and overcast but dry. Nicky made breakfast. I took Ted for a quick walk and then changed into my wedding clothes. The suit and unwashed shirt had been on a hanger in the wardrobe since the day Chris and I got married. We got into Georgie's car and she drove us to Westerleigh Crematorium.

It was about 11.30am when we arrived. People were gathering in the waiting room by the entrance to the crematorium. Peter walked over and put his arms around me: "How are you doing?"

I shrugged and said nothing. If I opened my mouth to speak, I would shatter like a dropped vase. "Everything's fine," he said. "It's going to be a lovely service. We'll do her proud."

My oldest son Jamie arrived and greeted me with a bear hug. He's 6'2" and broad-shouldered. For a full minute I relaxed into my son's arms. Then Jamie released his grip and stood back. "Fucker, eh?" he said.

I nodded, tears in my eyes.

Guests came over to say hello and offer their condolences. I responded as well as I could but had few words. My daughters stood close by like bodyguards, keeping a watchful eye on me, protecting me from too much attention.

At midday, a green hearse pulled up. Jeremy Clutterbuck and his dark-suited staff opened the back of the hearse and slid the coffin out onto their linked arms. It was made of plain compressed cardboard, with no handles. The top was festooned with fresh-picked hedgerow foliage with small pots of white hellebores dotted among the greenery.

At Jeremy's nod, the pall bearers lifted the coffin onto their shoulders in a single synchronised movement. They paused, checked their balance and walked slowly through the open double doors into the chapel. As they made their way towards the catafalque at the far end of the aisle, we followed behind.

Karl Jenkins' *Benedictus* played as we entered and took our places in the pews. Chris and I had listened to it together at the Penny Brohn Cancer Care Centre, less than two weeks before she died, sitting side by side, holding hands under a blanket. We had wept together then, knowing what was to come. The memory of that moment undid me completely. A torrent of grief ripped through me and I sobbed uncontrollably. Nicky and Georgie put their arms around me and Jamie stretched out a hand and gripped mine, until my sobs subsided.

Through my tears, I could just make out the picture, on an easel near the coffin, of Chris floating in the shallows of a lake. She was wearing a sun hat and a broad smile on her face. I remembered taking the photograph when we visited Minnesota to see black bears. We'd spent the whole day canoeing round that lake; had a picnic lunch on a small island; jumped off the rocks and skinny-dipped; dozed and made love naked in the sun; seen a bald eagle hunting for prey and heard a loon calling. I hugged this secret knowledge to my chest.

Then Peter's voice called me back to the present. He was standing behind the lectern and announced that the service would begin with a reading of some of Chris's own words. Our old friend Tracy Goldsmith took his place at the microphone. Her eyes were full of tears and it took a few moments for her to find her voice. "Chris and Geoff had just got married when she wrote these words last January," she said.

> Perhaps we yearn for an impossible dream, to belong here and now, to each other, to be the roots and the soil, to grow from place and tribe, to go out and perform as a troupe performs and return home to be greeted and fed and then to sleep.
>
> My home is now, during my turn on the planet, passing through with this tribe – this troupe of wonderful creative, vital people alive at a time of astonishing loss.

We sat in silence for a little while, seeing the image of Chris herself behind the words, which seemed to capture the essence of her vibrant presence in the world. I was very glad we'd started with them. Then Peter read the poem "We Who Love You" that I had written for Chris the morning she had her biopsy operation.

When those wyrd sisters dreamt the web
of your fate, they laboured long and hard.
Artfully they chose the matter of your life:
friendship, love, intelligence – and delight.

Round the golden spindle of your name
they spun you into being: they braided
the strings that marry you to this world,
and gave the threads to all of us to hold.

We will not let you go alone into the night
for we are woven into the selfsame cloth,
the warp and the weft of a single tapestry.
Our love will keep you always in the light.

As I heard Peter reading my words, I remembered the day of the biopsy. Chris had stayed overnight on the neurosurgery ward at Southmeads Hospital and I'd got up very early, written the poem and driven to be with her for the day. She had been hungry but in good spirits when I arrived.

"Today's the day," I'd said.

"It's an experience," she replied.

"What do you mean?"

"I'm going to make the most of it."

I still hadn't quite understood what she meant, but she seemed calm and I decided not to press for more. "I've written a poem for you," I said.

"Read it to me," she said. "I like to hear you read."

I read her the poem and hand her the printed copy to keep.

"It's lovely. Thank you," she said.

I'd stayed by her side until the porter came to wheel her away to prepare for the operation, then I checked at the nurses' station to make sure they'd got my mobile number. "What do I do now?" I asked.

"There's a private lounge on the landing," said the nurse at the desk. "We'll call you when it's over."

I got a coffee from the kiosk and made my way to the lounge. I sat on a sofa and looked round. Just me and a clock on the wall. It was 12.15pm. I got out a book and tried to read. The print blurred after a few minutes and I gave up. Nothing to do but wait.

At 4.17pm, my mobile phone rang.

"Mr Mead?"

"Yes."

"Dr Faulkner here from the neurosurgery team. She's in Recovery."

"How is she?"

"Good as new. No damage done. We've got the samples. She's resting down here for a little while then we'll send her back up to the ward."

"Thank you," I said. Relief flooded through me.

"Really, she's fine," said Dr Faulkner. I guessed he had heard the catch in my voice. "In fact, she's quite remarkable. She actually walked into the operating theatre chatting to the anaesthetist. I've never seen anything like it."

"That's my girl," I'd said, and put the phone down.

I smiled with the memory of being told how she had sashayed into the operating theatre. Then I brought my attention back to the service; it was time for the next reading. It was the turn of our friend William Ayot who, with his wife Juliet, had officiated at our wedding just 12 months before. William is a consummate and well-published poet. He'd written "At the Last Leaf's Edge" in Chris's memory:

And after the storm, a final descent –
falling like a raindrop from leaf to leaf,
building momentum and gathering weight,
to plummet and splash, collide and dissolve,
only to re-form and fall again –
her grief and denial, terror and rage,
tumbling through layers of light and greenery,
each its own world of transformative loss –
changing and shape-shifting, becoming other,
yet still a discernible bead of water;
trickling downward to the last leaf's edge,
where she finally tips into infinite space;
and finds herself, one tear amongst millions,
glittering and shining in the failing light,
seeking the ground of her last becoming;
made and remade, purified and polished,
perfected and falling...falling...falling...

Then, as the sound of Leonard Cohen singing "Here It Is" filled the chapel, Peter invited us to take a marker pen and write or draw our last messages to Chris on the coffin. Our tears mixed with laughter as we gathered round and scribbled, doodled and made marks.

Liz and Wendy, the women from the agency who had cared for Chris daily after her return home from hospital, giggled as they drew a crossed-out pink bra. "She'll be pleased not to be struggling with that any more," Wendy whispered in my ear.

I stood by the coffin, not knowing what to write until I recalled the story I wrote for her when she was in hospital. I had wanted to give her an image of death and dying that she could embrace, and had written a story about a girl who was half-human and half-bear. I found a blank space and scrawled *Sleep in the arms of the Great Bear. Play among the stars. Goodbye sweetheart. I love you.* As the words flowed from the pen, I laughed through my tears and I realised that I'd written the story as much for my benefit as hers.

When we had all finished, we returned to our seats. Carole Bond, one of Chris's oldest friends, led us in a chorus of, "Amen." As we sang, the curtain closed in front of the catafalque, hiding the coffin from view, and Chris went from us forever. I looked around as we sat down. Many guests were weeping; some were holding each other. The sudden finality of her disappearance seemed to have caught us all unawares.

Gradually though, the energy shifted. Sue Hollingsworth went to the lectern to read a poem called "Words for Chris After Fire" written by our friend Robert McNeer who lives in Italy and couldn't come to the funeral.

Sue swept her gaze over the congregation, gathering us in, bringing us back into each other's presence. Her face relaxed into a wide smile. "This is a clown poem," she said, "a love letter from one clown to another. I feel as though I should be wearing a red nose."

She lifted the paper from the lectern and as she opened her mouth to speak, another friend, Chris Nichols, jumped up from his pew: "I've got one here," he said, fishing a clown nose from his pocket and handing it to Sue. She pulled the elastic over her head, wriggled the red rubber nose into position, and replaced her reading glasses. "That's much better," she said and launched into the poem with gusto.

O Chris!
Hey, Ho, Hi!
And Higher, even,
Burn the Fire!

How to address you now,
Darling Chuck? Princess Pumpkin?
What pitch will reach, what name find you,
From this our cold cold ground?
Your laughter's still in my ears, Soul Buddy,
and Now,

Spirit Sister,
Sweet, Silly One:
A clown's Clown, now,
Smiling in your great
Igloo of Light,

Forgive me, please, these words:
Clumsy arrows, that do,
I trust, no harm.
Know that they Burn with Love,
They Fly with Gratitude.
They say what they can, while they can,
Before rattling back to earth.

I know that the pure
Beauty of your Being
Cannot be parsed.

You inhabit, now, something Complete in Itself.
This is your Art, now, this your Beauty.

Thank you, Chris,
Your life has changed us,
Your Art is through Us, now:

We Burn Now,
Brighter, Greater,
Because of you.

Thank you, Chris,
And again,
Thank you.

I smiled with pleasure, remembering the times Chris and I had travelled to Puglia to clown with Robert at his theatre school, and then it occurred to me that we'd never do that – or anything else together – again. Sue finished reading and returned the red nose. Peter closed the service and we left the chapel, just as Chris and I had left the registry office when we got married, to the sound of Penguin Café Orchestra playing "Perpetuum Mobile."

Looking back, the rest of the day is a blur. I remember that we all went to the Bodkin Hotel; a log fire burned in the grate; there were sandwiches and tea and cakes; friends and relatives said nice things about Chris and wished me well. I've no idea what they said or what I said in reply; I felt like I was sleepwalking. There was someone else in the room who walked and talked exactly like me; he shook people's hands, said hello and thank you and good to see you. But that wasn't me; I was elsewhere, with Chris by the lake in Minnesota.

It wasn't until I got home that evening that my head cleared and I was able to look back on the day and take in what had happened. Peter had encouraged me to follow my instincts about the service and together we had, indeed, done Chris proud. I'd got a glimpse of how important it would be to respond artfully to grief and bereavement. I'd seen Chris live and die artfully, with curiosity, passion and creativity. She had taught me much during our time together but I still had a lot to learn.

For the first time, I allowed myself to contemplate what was to come. I'd have to get back to earning a living, and there would be her will and all the legal stuff to sort out; her memorial to install; a celebration to organise; her books and clothes to give away; her art materials and pictures to find homes for; her ashes to scatter. Her ashes: Christ, I'd forgotten about them. The reality of her cremation suddenly hit me. She was gone, her flame-coloured silk wedding dress vaporised, her body consumed in the fire.

The physical space she had occupied in the world was now a void, like those left behind by the figures caught in the volcanic eruption in Pompeii, where we had been on holiday a few years before. For years, my life had been shaped by her presence. Now, I realised, it would be shaped by her absence. The pain of that realisation tore at my heart and I wept.

Ted came over to see what was the matter, as he always did when I was upset. He pawed at my knees, asking to come up. I drew him onto my lap and hugged him with both arms. He looked straight at me with those dark soulful eyes and then snuffled his wet nose into my neck, as if to say, "You're not alone. I love you. We'll be alright."

I wasn't so sure, but Chris had told me once that dogs never lie. I stopped crying, put on my coat, got Ted's lead and took him out for a last moonlit walk before bed. As he trotted faithfully by my side along the lane, I looked up at the stars and began to feel lighter. She had gone but she was still there.

"Goodnight sweetheart," I called out. "Thank you."

CHAPTER 4

INTO THE VOID

"All sorrows can be borne if you put them in a story or tell a story about them," said Karen Blixen who wrote *Out of Africa*. She knew a thing or two about sorrow, having lost her father to suicide, her husband to divorce, her health to syphilis, her lover to a flying accident, and her beloved Kenyan farm to bankruptcy. Like Blixen, I write because the story is all I have and telling it is the only way I know to bear the sorrow.

Karen Karp, a longtime friend of Chris's and mine, reminded me of the quotation when she sent me a *New York Times* article by psychotherapist Patrick O'Malley, ironically called "Getting Grief Right." He points out that the so-called stages of grief (shock, denial, anger, bargaining, depression and acceptance) have become a dangerous kind of orthodoxy. Trying to measure the progress of our grief against this yardstick creates a false expectation that it can be contained or managed. Rather, he says:

> When loss is a story, there is no right or wrong way to grieve. There is no pressure to move on. There is no shame in intensity or duration. Sadness, regret, confusion, yearning and all the experiences of grief become part of the narrative of love for the one who died.

I am learning that things do change but also that the process of grief does not follow a predictable path: the heart is ruled by *kairos* not *chronos*. One day I notice the sunlight, the next all seems dark; one moment I laugh, the next cry; I curse and pray in the same breath.

My heart was attuned to yearning early in my life with the death of my father. I grew up with a tacit belief, which took many decades to dispel, that love and absence were synonymous. It took years of living with Chris finally to learn that it was possible to love someone who was present. Nevertheless, there was a kind of familiarity about the intense feelings of longing that arose when Chris died. Her death recapitulated all the losses I had ever known.

As a child I believed that if I missed my father enough, he would return. As young children do, particularly if they are left to manage their grief on their own, I blamed myself for his absence. If only I'd loved him more he wouldn't have died; if I missed him enough he would come back to life. It's the kind of magical thinking that bereavement spawns both in children and adults.

And as a child, I kept those feelings to myself because to speak them aloud would rob them of their magical power. When Chris died, I realised how easy it would be for me to revert to this deeply ingrained and self-destructive pattern, and determined that the best way I could help myself would be to find ways of expressing my grief. Writing a memoir of Chris's illness and death, blogging about my life as a widower, and writing poetry have been my attempts to pay exquisite attention to the sadness, regret, confusion and yearning to which O'Malley refers. To impose too much order on this material retrospectively would be both dishonest and misleading. The luxurious logic of hindsight is not available in the midst of experience. As Soren Kierkegaard once said, "Life must be remembered backward, but lived forward." So, I shall stay close to the reality and confusion of lived experience, dating blog posts to show when they were written, and allowing the story to unfold messily on the page.

When Chris died I felt as though I had fallen into a void. For several months after the funeral, I tried unsuccessfully to dull the pain by working too hard and drinking too much, until one day I realised that unless I could resist the narcotic lure of overwork and alcohol and gaze into the void itself, I would never find life and meaning again. I remembered a favourite joke that I used to share with Chris that expressed the dilemma beautifully.

A man is walking along the highway of his life. One day, without any warning, he falls into an existential abyss. It's dark, precipitous and terrifying. He can't see the bottom and he's clinging to the vertical sides by his fingernails.

He is utterly alone.

After a while he can't bear the loneliness and calls out into the darkness:

"Is there anybody there?"

"Yes," booms an enormous voice across the void. "I am here with you."

"Who are you?" calls the man.

"I am God," replies the voice.

"What should I do?" says the man, looking down. "Tell me what to do."

"Let go," says God.

There is a long pause before the man calls again:

"Is there anybody else?"

I had decided to gaze into the void, but I'd already fallen into the abyss. The question I had to ask myself now was whether to cling on limpet-like to what was left of the familiar, comforting routines of my life or let myself fall into the unknown. I knew what Chris would have said. I could almost hear her welcoming voice rising up from below and echoing round me:

"What are you waiting for?"

SWEETHEART COME
22 DECEMBER 2014

My left foot is suddenly painful. I take off my shoe carefully. The nails have penetrated the sole of the shoe and raked my instep. There is blood. I hear my name being called softly; a seductive female voice, rising and falling, squeezing a siren song from its monosyllabic form: "G-e-o-ff."

It's a dream.

I wake up in your bed.

Not the second-best bed that Shakespeare left his wife, but your second (best) bed; the bed you bought for yourself just before we met; the bed that had been intended to celebrate your new-found aloneness; the bed in which we slept, made love, argued over the duvet, drank tea, laughed, talked into the night, made plans and dreamt of a life together. The bed that was too small for two people to sleep in comfortably. The bed we moved into the sitting room when you could no longer climb the stairs.

I'm alone in the house apart from Ted who is curled up on the floor between me and the doorway to the kitchen. He sticks closer to me these days, now that you've gone. The house creaks and groans as a winter storm lashes the trees in the garden and curls around the old stones. I listen carefully. Was it your voice I heard? If so, you are silent now.

I reach out for the alarm clock and bring it close to my face. Without my glasses, it's hard to make out the exact position of the hands. I guess that it's about 5.30 in the morning. Yesterday was the winter solstice, the shortest day of the year. It's pitch black outside. I turn on the light, step over Ted – who glances up at me and thumps his tail three or four times on the carpet – and make my way into the kitchen. I'm still half asleep; I make a mug of tea, bring it back to bed and think of you.

Portugal. August 2013. The first big seizure. The brutal diagnosis. "Inoperable," they said in broken English. We sat in the hospital corridor, unable to move, for what seemed like hours. Suddenly, I looked at you and saw you gazing back at me. All the ifs and buts and maybes that had characterised our relationship simply melted away.

"Will you marry me?" I said.

"Yes," you said.

Five words. That's all it took, after a decade of dithering, to seal the bond between us. Love spoke and we obeyed its call.

No champagne, no flowers, no extravagant gestures. Just two people weeping for joy in the face of disaster. And four months later came the wedding: the public declaration and ongoing private commitments of marriage.

I lean back on the pillows of the bed in which you died not three weeks ago, and let the memories of our wedding suffuse my slow waking into the day. Imprinted on my heart is the glory of you, radiant in your flame silk dress, as our families and friends sing "Sweetheart Come" and bind our hands together with a hundred multi-coloured ribbons.

GAME OVER
4 JANUARY 2015

"Game over," you would say when you talked of death, when you talked of death at all, which was rarely, preferring to talk about life and living it until the end. Game over because, for you, dear Chris, play was the essence of life.

You told me once that Japanese verbs conjugate in a variety of forms with the highest reserved exclusively for the Emperor. The Emperor doesn't converse or fight or write verse, you said, he plays at conversing, plays at fighting, and plays at writing verse. I've no idea where you got that from or whether it's true but I do remember that you told me with a delighted and defiant grin.

I've never known anyone more playful than you or more in love with life. Teaching, facilitating, skiing, running, painting, cooking, dressing up, making love, getting married were all opportunities to be playful, to be creative, and to be exuberantly delighted. And I was blessed for a dozen years to play alongside you. "My mate," you called me: your partner and your playmate.

Now you have gone – jumped over the hedge at the end of the garden, as our friend Adrian put it – and I am left playing solitaire. But I am still playing; you taught me that much.

As for "game over," I'm not so sure. I have no religious faith but I trust the wisdom of my heart and I cannot believe that your unquenchable spirit will ever stop playing, if not on this level then the next.

I'LL MEET YOU THERE
7 FEBRUARY 2015

That Chris lived and died artfully is both glorious and poignant. Glorious because she continues to inspire me and many others to do likewise and poignant because I am surrounded by the artefacts – the books, papers, journals, images, clothes, furniture, fabrics, trinkets and decorations – through which she expressed herself. I will tidy the house one day, maybe even change things round a bit, but right now I don't want to do anything that might dilute or diminish the sense I have of being in her presence. In the meantime, I wonder how best to stay connected to the vibrant being that I so loved.

Hmmm. I notice that I used the past tense for love, maybe because despite all that I still love about her, I can no longer love her embodied womanly self. That physical aspect of her has gone from the world. But I wonder, what else of her remains? To whom or to what am I speaking when I light a candle and tell her how much I miss her?

If I believe anything, it is that Chris lives on in us through our memories of her, the ways in which she challenged and changed us, and through something more elusive yet enduring that we might call her essence or spirit. To claim to know what this is with any certainty would somehow diminish the awesome mystery of life and death that I have experienced in the last few weeks and months. What I want is not to pretend to understand this mystery but to learn how to participate in it more fully.

When I really want to feel connected with Chris, I either turn to my own artful practice as a writer or else to the poetry of someone like that great spiritual seeker Rumi, especially when it's a poem that we found together and both loved.

> Out beyond ideas of wrongdoing and rightdoing,
> there is a field. I'll meet you there.
>
> When the soul lies down in that grass,
> the world is too full to talk about.
> Ideas, language, even the phrase *each other*
> doesn't make any sense.

ALHAMBRA NIGHTS
16 FEBRUARY 2015

I've come to Spain, to the mountains of the Sierra Nevada, for a short writing retreat: my first trip away since Chris died. I stayed overnight in Granada in a hotel beneath the ramparts of the Alhambra Palace. Wandering into the city to find somewhere for a solitary dinner, I found myself outside a restaurant called La Gran Taverna. Chris and I had eaten there a few years previously and as I stared at the condensation-misted window, I saw her looking back at me. It was as though, for a few magical moments, she had come back to see me. Her image faded, but I could sense her presence all around me and I walked through the Plaza Nueva as if my feet were dancing.

We came here once,
footloose for a day,
to wander in the city.

Now I'm on my own
and passing through
to somewhere else.

I walk to Plaza Nueva
past La Gran Taverna
and stop in my tracks.

Your smiling face hangs
in the misty window
next to my reflection.

"Don't you remember?
It's not so long ago,"
you seem to say.

"We had dinner here
and laughed so much
we could hardly eat.

That was a good day.
But it was *before*.
I wish I could stay."

I blow you a kiss
>> as your face fades away,
>>> leaving the scent of your hair.

There's magic in the moonlit air;
>> I look around the bustling square
>>> and suddenly you're everywhere.

THE TANGO LESSON
7 MARCH 2015

A few years ago, Chris came back from a trip to South America, raving about an impromptu tango evening she had been taken to by her hosts. "There were all shapes and sizes, young and old," she said. "The men came up and asked me to dance. I didn't know I could do it but they led brilliantly and made me feel so graceful."

My own dance repertoire being limited to head banging and a rather pale imitation of John Travolta, I let her comment pass. But when she followed up in the next few weeks by renting DVDs of Sally Potter's *The Tango Lesson* and of Al Pacino strutting his stuff in *Scent of a Woman*, I took the hint and booked a half-day tango lesson for us both as a surprise birthday present.

Sadly, my two left feet combined with Chris's absolute refusal (in practice, if not in theory) to allow me to lead her anywhere left us both frustrated and footsore. Nevertheless, we bought some fancy tango shoes and determined to give it another go. A couple of sessions later, however, the reality of my incompetence on the dance floor overcame any remaining *Strictly Come Dancing* fantasies.

We put away our tango shoes for good. "Well, at least we gave it a go," said Chris, finding a crumb of comfort in the fact that I had been willing to suffer public humiliation for her benefit.

"I'm not sure those shoes were good for your feet," was all I could think to say.

But Chris continued to dance with life, through images, ideas, words and deeds. She brought the same playful impulse to her art and her work, making no real distinction between them. She danced with her illness and, in the end, she danced with death.

She understood, as Susan Sontag wrote in *Illness as Metaphor*, that the metaphors we use to describe our illness come to define us. Wisely, she refused to frame her condition as a battle against cancer. "How can you fight something that is part of yourself?" she once said. "This is about living well and looking after myself; about doing what I love and being myself, whatever the circumstances."

So instead of fighting her illness, she allowed it to lead her, responding to every improvised step with the verve, intelligence and spirit of a true *tanguera*: a mistress of tango.

100 Days
21 March 2015

Last week, I realised that a hundred days had gone by since Chris died. This milestone made me think of what business and self-help gurus say about our supposed ability to change the world and ourselves in such a short period. I've always distrusted gurus and I believe that this kind of wishful thinking is an unhelpful fantasy. Life, love and loss seem to go at their own pace.

> Anything is possible,
> The new-age gurus say.
>
> 100 days is time enough
> To turn your life around,

To seek a new direction,
To find another ground.

But time is out of kilter,
You've stilled the hourglass.

How can I plan a future
When you are in the past?

There's nowhere that I want to go
Without you by my side

And nothing that I want to do
If you can't do it too.

To those who tell us otherwise
I have some news for you:

100 days is not enough
To make a life anew.

WELL OF GRIEF
17 APRIL 2015

In a beautiful turn of phrase, poet David Whyte invites us to slip beneath the still surface of the well of grief and descend through the blackness to find a secret source of cold clear water from which to drink.

The metaphor is apt; each time I turn to the page to write about Chris, I visit this well. I know that its waters nourish me but, at first sight, they are black and uninviting. Each time I ask myself, "Do I really have to go there again?" and then, "Should I drink? Shall I jump in? Will I drown?"

People do drown in wells and sometimes in despair but shedding the hot tears and drinking the cold clear waters of grief seem to nourish and restore us. Why should this be? Perhaps because grief is not just a personal affliction. We all visit the well from time to time and, in a close-knit community, when one weeps all weep; when one drinks, all drink.

Chris had an extraordinary capacity for building and fostering community: a web of relationships criss-crossing the world. This enduring community of friendship that now sustains and supports me is her last and perhaps her greatest gift.

This Clay Jug
20 May 2015

This morning, I caught myself laying two places for breakfast. I put one set of cutlery in front of me and only then did I notice the spare knife and fork still in my hand. It wasn't until I reached out to put them down opposite me on the table that reality kicked in.

"She's not here."

For 15 years, Chris and I fought and loved and struggled; we are inextricably entwined; there is no part of my life untouched by her spirit. Yet I cannot reach out and take her hand; I cannot hold her in the night; we cannot laugh together, make plans together, talk together, dream together. I cannot call her on the phone to commiserate when something goes wrong, or to celebrate a successful venture. I see her wherever I turn, but she is not here.

I was trying to explain this duality of her presence and absence to a friend: "It's like that poem by Kabir. The one about the clay jug. It contains all the wonders of the universe, but sometimes you just want to feel the earthy warmth and soft contours of the clay."

The Sea, The Sea
14 June 2015

"How are you, Geoff?"

It's the question everybody asks. Of course they do. They want to know.

"I'm good," I reply. "If good includes bad."

I work. I exercise (not enough). I eat and drink (a bit too much). I sit at the keyboard writing and re-writing the story of the past two years to make my sorrow bearable. I pour my energy into creating a celebration of Chris's life. I fill my days. I numb myself in the evenings with good wine and old movies. I sleep. I worry that two houses, an office, a sports car, a saloon car and a camper van are not sustainable on one rather dented income but can't bring myself to let anything go. I laugh sometimes. I cry often. I love my dog.

"How are you, Geoff?"

There are a million ways to answer that one. The real question is much more difficult. It's not *how* it's *who*?

"Who are you, Geoff? Who are you now?"

And the truth is that I don't know who I am. I knew who I was when I was Chris's lover, then partner, then husband. I have no idea who I am now that she's gone. In some ways I'm still her husband: we're still "married" on Facebook; I still wear my wedding ring; I still love her. That she loved me, I have no doubt. But how can I be her beloved when she isn't here?

Is this what it is to be widowed? To live in a world where time's arrow no longer flies true? To know oneself by who one used to be? To bask in the afterglow of having been loved while aching for the one who is lost, like a beached whale trying to ease its suffering with memories of the ocean?

CHAPTER 5

CURATING A LIFE

In February 2015, I emailed family members and as many friends and colleagues of Chris's that I could bring to mind with this invitation to a celebration of her life to be held at the end of June at Matara, a wonderful Regency house and gardens, just a few hundred yards from Folly Cottage, where we got married in December 2013 and where Chris's memorial now stands.

> Please come and help us celebrate the many aspects of Chris's remarkably creative life: artist, teacher, ecologist, clown, writer, intellectual, ursophile, dog lover, bookaholic, sister, daughter, friend, partner, mentor, catalyst, designer...
>
> We will be coming together for two days of exhibitions, installations, food rituals, music, clowning, storytelling, conversation, artful activities, sharing memories, poetry, quiet contemplation, and whatever else we can come up with. Do let me know if you have any ideas or would like to contribute in some way.
>
> Each day will offer a range of activities and you are welcome to come for one or both days. There will be a "grazing bar" for tea, coffee and snacks throughout and something a bit more substantial at lunchtimes. Ask me for a list of local B&Bs and hotels if you need overnight accommodation. We are also hoping to have a "Skype Corner" so that folk who cannot come, especially from overseas, can connect with us during the event.
>
> The event is by invitation and request. Chris had a huge circle of friends and colleagues and I'm bound to miss some of you by mistake so if you don't receive an invitation directly from me, know that you too are welcome. Also please feel free to pass on the invitation to anyone else you think might like to come.

Before she died, Chris had asked me to arrange a "bang-up celebration" of her life and I was determined to create a memorable happening. She had been a gregarious extrovert with a rare gift for collaboration and friendship, and I realised that the best way of creating such an event would be to co-create it with others. First, I made sure that the invitation asked everyone for ideas and contributions and very soon I spoke with Christopher Goscomb, a dear friend whose doctoral inquiry into "making and exhibiting" Chris had supervised. Who better to curate a celebration of Chris's artful life?

Christopher asked me who else it would be good to involve in planning the event and suggested an early meeting at Folly Cottage to get the ball rolling. A few weeks later, a small group of us were sitting around the kitchen table shaping a long wish list of potential exhibits and activities into a two-day extravaganza. Before long, we had designed a layout for the exhibition and loosely organised a programme of music, poetry, art-making and storytelling.

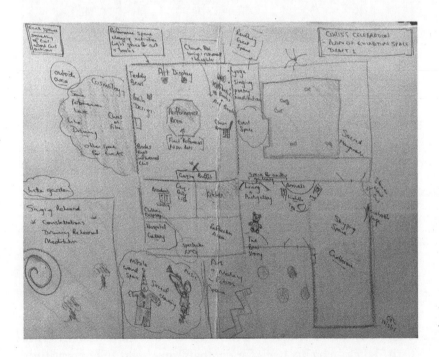

I recall many particular moments: pulling together the written tributes and poems sent by Chris's friends and admirers; selecting and framing her drawings and paintings for display; collating her journals and academic writing; working with friends to realise a large artwork that Chris had designed to represent aspects of her experience in hospital; borrowing mannequins and dressing them in Chris's clothes.

In the end, some two hundred people came either for one or both days to take part in the celebration. Most arrived looking solemn and left with a smile on their face. With Christopher's help, we had created a convivial and memorable event of the kind that we knew Chris would have wanted. We had not come together passively to pay our respects but to engage actively with Chris's artful life and with each other as a community united by our common grief and the many ways in which we loved her.

I wanted Chris, not me, to be the centre of attention and tried to stay in the background as much as possible once the event got under way, wandering round the various exhibitions and activities with Ted close by my heels for company, my heart full of gratitude and a sense of satisfaction that I'd fulfilled the promise I had made to Chris for a "bang-up celebration."

It was good to see so many people from different parts of her life come together: old friends deep in conversation; new connections being made; laughter as well as tears as stories were shared. Chris felt very present: the visible fruits of her life all around us in the artefacts and in the relationships she had enjoyed and fostered wherever she went. For two days, it was as though she was still with us and I dreaded them coming to an end.

As the final afternoon drew to a close, the 30 or 40 people still remaining gathered in the main room to say farewell. Our friend Carole, a jazz singer, had written a song for Chris called "Time for Tea" as a gift before she died and sang it as we sat around on the floor. Its lyrics evoked the essence of Chris so perfectly that we wept to hear them and I'm writing them now through fresh tears.

What is life, she said, if not extraordinary?
What is love, she said, if not sublime?
What is art, she said, if not pure alchemy?
What is truth, she said, but simply a matter of time?
Simply a matter of time.

And she will smile and she will chuckle,
And she will throw back her head and laugh...and say
Over the hill there are bears and butterflies
Over the next one I'll ski
Down in the valley there are clowns and camper vans
And the dogs will come home in time for tea
Yes, the dogs will follow us home.

Use your ears, she said, the world is calling to you
See in touch, she said, speak in mime
Climb your hill, she said, and then enjoy the view
You'll find grace, she said, it's simply a matter of time
Simply a matter of time.

And she will smile and she will chuckle
And she will throw her head back and laugh...and say
Over the hill there are paints and storybooks
Over the next one I'll dance
Down in the valley there are tents and firesides
And the dogs will come home in time for tea
Yes, the dogs will follow us home.

When we're born, she said, we are extraordinary
We can search, she said, for the sublime
Make our lives, she said, an act of alchemy
We're all light, she said, it's simply a matter of time
Simply a matter of time

And she will smile and she will chuckle,
And throw back her head and laugh…and say
Over the hill there are cakes and chocolate
Over the next one I'll sing
Down in the valley is the meaning and mystery
And the dogs will come home in time for tea
Yes, the dogs will follow us home.

And the dogs will come home in time for tea
Yes, the dogs will follow us home.

When planning the celebration, we'd decided that it should end with cake and champagne. While they were being served, two musician friends, Jed and Fergal, sang a version of Nick Cage's beautiful song "Sweetheart Come." Jed had sung it at our wedding just 18 months before. I'd arranged it as a surprise for Chris to be serenaded by the whole congregation as she came into the chamber for the marriage ceremony. I had struggled then to sing through tears of joy and now my voice cracked with grief and my tears flowed freely.

As the final chorus ended, we raised our glasses and a friend asked, "Do you want to say something, Geoff?" I nodded and all eyes seemed to turn towards me as I fought to find my voice. I had known this was coming and had decided I would say what felt right in the moment rather than prepare anything in advance. I wanted Chris herself to be heard in the room and reached for one of the photographs we'd had printed as mementos, on the back of which were printed her words that we had read at her cremation service. I breathed slowly and opened my mouth, wondering what would come out. I could only just speak but pressed on, buoyed up by the thought that she deserved a proper farewell toast.

"Chris was my girl. I loved her but she did not belong to me. She was a much bigger person than that. She belonged to the world and her sense of belonging included all of us in this room and many more besides. These are her words, written soon after we got married here in this very room, less than a year before she died.

Perhaps we yearn for an impossible dream, to belong here and now, to each other, to be the roots and the soil, to grow from place and tribe, to go out and perform as a troupe performs and return home to be greeted and fed and then to sleep.

My home is now, during my turn on the planet, passing through with this tribe – this troupe of wonderful, creative, vital people – alive at a time of astonishing loss.

"Thank you Chris, for a life well lived, for your love and friendship, and for everything you taught us."

Then we drank our champagne and ate our cake with gusto, as Chris would have wanted, before saying goodbye to each other and making our way home. I couldn't bear to see the exhibits being taken down, and sat outside in the afternoon sunlight with my eyes half closed and Ted on my lap as a gang of friends took care of everything.

It dawned on me that now the celebration was over, I would have to find a new focus for my energy. As an introvert, I knew that I would need to spend some time on my own and felt pleased that Ted and I would soon be going to France in the camper van for five weeks. Before that, however, I'd planned a short trip to Crete, and began to think about taking some of Chris's ashes to a certain spot that we had both loved. Time would tell me what to do, I mused.

Over the next few days, as the significance of the celebration really sank in, I wrote two blog posts which are reproduced below, and some of us who had been to the celebration shared photographs and music as a permanent record of the event on a special Facebook page entitled "An Artful Life." Anyone who wants to get more of a feeling for the two days is welcome to visit the page and click through the various images and galleries.

LIGHT BREAKS THROUGH
2 JULY 2015

It rained on Sunday; on Wednesday it was overcast and humid. But on Monday and Tuesday the weather was perfect. Kingscote basked in bright sunlight.

We danced, drummed and sang. We shared stories; listened to music; read Chris's journals; dived into her gloriously iconoclastic academic writing; gazed in wonder at her pictures and sketch books; enjoyed displays of her iconic outfits; talked about cosmology; cuddled teddy bears; looked at pictures from her childhood; wrote poetry; explored deep time; painted and drew; sat with old friends; made new connections; laughed, cried, and ate cake.

All this came about through the efforts of Chris's family and friends, sparked by their love for this remarkable woman and gratitude for a life lived with such generosity and brilliance. Convening and preparing for the celebration was a source of great joy, though I sometimes found it a bit overwhelming and difficult to stay present during the event itself.

On Monday afternoon I needed to escape for a while so I went to the meditation room with Ted and slept for an hour, until a friend came in and hugged us both awake as if we had been Sleeping Beauties. In that moment, I felt a surge of erotic energy returning to my body and I began to imagine the concrete possibility of life beyond the celebration for the first time since Chris died.

I realised that the energy I'd poured into making the event happen was a way of keeping her alive. Now it's over, I have to let her go. It's hard and the way ahead looks dark. But as our friend Fergal O'Connor says in the title track of his new album: light has a habit of breaking through.

TIME BIDS BE GONE
5 JULY 2015

I took this picture when I went to Andalucía in February. I walked the same mountain trail several times. Clinging to a ledge at its highest point was the twisted remnant of a tree, blasted by lightning. The sun glinted on its stark beauty; its limbs framed the living mountains. But its hollowed trunk was quite empty. Its charred branches would never bud or blossom again.

Until Matara, I felt alive, though living in a kind of void. I poured my love and energy into creating a glorious celebration of Chris's life. What I hadn't realised was that when it ended, so too would the magical thinking that was keeping Chris alive inside me.

When all her pictures were taken down, her journals packed away, and the stuff of her life disassembled, the void in which I had been living entered my body and hollowed me out.

For the first time, I feel empty inside.

When I realise that she has truly gone, I can't stand up. I fall to the kitchen floor and howl like a wounded animal. Words escape my mouth, unbidden: "What's the point? What's the fucking point?"

Ted rushes over and shoves his chops in mine. He licks the snot and tears from my face, bathes me in his hot sweet breath, and brings his furry body as close to mine as possible. I put my arms around him and weep into his neck. He wuffles and grunts as if to say, "It's OK, I'm here."

We're a pack (albeit a pack of two) and he knows that's what you do when a member of your pack is in that kind of trouble. The emptiness recedes and I slowly come back to life.

I give Ted a hug and rub his coat. Job done, he slips out of my arms and wanders off into the garden to lie in wait for the postman. The kettle boils. I make a cup of tea and sit at the table, cradling the mug in both hands.

"I'm still here," I think. "She's gone but I'm still here."

It's enough for now.

CHAPTER 6

SOLITUDE

So many friends had been involved and so much effort had gone into planning and preparing the celebration in June that I wondered what would happen when it was all over. What would it be like without that clear focus for my energy, when I didn't have that event to look forward to? It was time to face the prospect of life without Chris and I had a hunch that I needed to be alone with my feelings for a while.

I decided to take Ted with me to France for five weeks over the summer in Rosie the camper van. Actually, her full name is Plastic Rosie since a string of plastic roses – bought in an Amsterdam flea market – festoon the dashboard. Chris and I bought her in October 2013 as an early wedding present to each other. As with so many good things in our life together, it was Chris's idea.

In 2014, we'd managed to get away for a week in Derbyshire over the Easter holiday and get a few long weekends in before the summer, when we expected to spend the whole of August in France. Those plans were abandoned when Chris fell ill and Rosie had sat motionless on the drive, attracting envious and admiring comments ever since. I wanted to make the trip that Chris and I had never managed, so I booked a place on the Portsmouth–Le Havre ferry and set off in late July, picking up my daughter Georgie en route as she had agreed to come with me for the first week to give me a "soft landing" as I ventured into a month of solitude.

I also wanted to deepen my practice as a writer over the summer. I had a couple of ideas for stories and I committed myself to documenting my sojourn in Brittany. Chris and I had spent an idyllic week there once, touring in our two-seater Morgan. I thought that revisiting old haunts would both bring me closer to her and force me to confront the reality of her absence. I began by looking at an old photograph to remind myself of the fun we'd had together a few years before.

We went to France my girl and me,
She wore my flying hat.
I've yet to be convinced, said she,
That I don't look a prat.

But you my sweet are on the road,
To wear it is your fate,
Adornment that is à la mode
Perched gaily on your pate.

You resemble Mr Gatsby,
She asseverated.
Very well then, let our hats be
Fashionably dated.

I'd written the poem as a gift for her at the time and told her how much I enjoyed the *Gatsby–hats be* rhyme. She laughed and insisted that I was too easily pleased by my own verse. But I noticed that she pinned it on the wall by her writing desk.

Those days were gone, I thought. We'd never wear silly hats or laugh together again. As the emotional roller-coaster of my solitary journey unfolded, I reflected on the high points and low points and recorded them in regular blog posts. Looking back on them now, I appreciate the unconscious wisdom that led me to give myself those uninterrupted weeks to focus on my grief and to mourn.

DESOLÉ
31 JULY 2015

A couple of days after we arrived at our first campsite, Georgie caught a train to Paris for the weekend. I dropped her at the station and went to the local Intermarché to get some supplies. I blundered around the over-stocked aisles until I came to the fruit and vegetables.

Suddenly I remembered how excited Chris would become at the abundance of fresh food in French supermarkets and reached for my iPhone to take a picture – as she would have done – of a display of enormous *coeur de boeuf* tomatoes. Local markets and village shops were her providers of choice, but she'd make an exception for a good Intermarché.

Everything had been an adventure with Chris; her curiosity and delight in the world were contagious. I filled the trolley with bottles of wine, apricots, *cuisses de poulet*, ham, cheese and croissants. But I felt more and more empty. She wasn't there to share any of this. I was so distracted that I dropped a jar of olives. It smashed on the floor and I went to find an assistant to clear it up.

"Pardon. Un petit accident. Je suis desolé."

I rolled the final phrase around in my mind and I thought, that's exactly how I feel. I'm not just sorry Chris isn't here, I feel desolated: abandoned, thoroughly alone. I went out to the car park in a black mood to load the camper van. Ted pounced on me with unconditional delight. He wagged his tail and buried his face in mine.

"Of course you're not alone," he seemed to say, "I'm here."

Merci beaucoup, mon ami.

MOON SONGS
1 AUGUST 2015

Last night there was a blue moon. That's to say, it was the second full moon of a month containing two full moons. There's a slightly more complicated version of a blue moon, which is the third full moon of an astronomical season containing four full moons. Anyway, it wasn't blue...which was a bit of a swizz.

When Chris was in hospital, the sterility of the environment troubled her and she was constantly looking for any connection she could make with the more-than-human world. One day she wrote in her journal:

I can see the moon passing by the window at night;

It was coral and cornflower blue just after dawn.

Now that's what I call a moon worth seeing, not that I would have noticed with my poor colour vision. Personally, I love a crescent moon hanging low and fat over the horizon. Then you can clearly see that it's not just a disc, but a three-dimensional sphere: our companion planet.

This year, Giffords Circus called their show Moon Songs. Chris and I adored Giffords and we used to go every year. For her

40th birthday, 40 of us had a champagne and strawberry picnic before the show and took over the whole of the Circus Sauce restaurant tent for dinner afterwards. When Tweedy the clown asked if it was anyone's birthday, a four-year-old, a six-year-old and Chris stuck up their hands. The whole audience sang "Happy Birthday."

Our friend Kathy Skerritt and I saw Moon Songs ten days ago. It was the first time I've been to see a Giffords show without Chris. I wanted to keep up the annual ritual but I couldn't bear to go on my own, so I was delighted that Kathy could join me. Chris would have loved it.

Seeing it was a bitter-sweet kind of sacrament.

LE BATEAU LIVRE
10 AUGUST 2015

Today I went back to Le Bateau Livre, a hidden gem near Penestin: a bookshop that is also a restaurant. Pascal Mucet and Marie-Paule Gaudin came up with this brilliant combination in 2005. I was last here four years ago, while on that holiday with Chris. We discovered it by chance as we drove along the coast road and loved it so much that we came back a couple of days later for a second look.

Much has changed since then but Pascal and Marie-Paule are just the same; their stock is still unusual and impossible to leave on the shelves; and l'assiette océane is still the best thing on a good menu. Being Sunday, free hors d'oeuvres and aperitifs were on hand for browsers. There's a lesson there for failing British independent bookshops, perhaps.

It was great to be back, though I noticed that my French deserted me entirely the moment I walked through the door so I guess something else was going on under the surface. I drove away from the shop, in the camper van with Ted in the passenger seat, closing his ears as I sang along to "Everybody Needs Somebody (To Love)" on the Atlantic Soul Greatest Hits CD.

I need you, you, you
I need you.

COLLYBONKER
13 AUGUST 2015

This magnificent erection is Rosie's drive-away awning (on a lovely campsite in the grounds of Château Lanniron in Quimper). It's a fantastically useful bit of kit which allows me and Ted to disgorge the contents of the camper van and leave them, safe and sound, while we drive off on adventures during the day.

I suspect Chris would think the awning was a bit *de trop* but I make no apologies: it does the job. Putting it up takes a while and the 30-plus tent pegs require liberal use of a good mallet. When we went camping, Chris and I always took a two-pound club hammer with us, which could drive a nail into concrete. For reasons that escaped me then and still elude me, she called said instrument a *collybonker*. It was undoubtedly useful but (as ultra-lightweight campers limited by the infinitesimal carrying capacity of the Morgan) we were concerned about both its bulk and weight. Our great – sadly unfulfilled – dream was to make our fortune by the invention of an inflatable collybonker.

THE GOOD, THE BAD AND THE UGLY
14 AUGUST 2015

It's been a mixed day today.

The good part was some nifty online detective work that tracked down a hotel Chris and I had stayed in at Douarnenez, four years ago, and then booking Ted and me in for one night next Monday. It has a private jacuzzi that Chris and I enjoyed during our visit. I'm pretty sure everyone makes love in it but you try not to think about the previous couple as you lock the door and slip under the bubbles.

The bad part was the pissing rain and being trapped inside a small camper van with a wet, frustrated dog. I did a bit of client work and translated a short Breton mermaid story (which wasn't so bad, I guess) but I still felt stir crazy by about 4.00pm. I hung on until nearly 6.00pm before cracking open the whisky and managed not to get legless. That word looks odd, should it be Legolas? Nope, he was an elf. Legless it is then.

The ugly part is the rage I feel at Chris for inflicting this bloody empty existence on me. They say that anger is a stage of grief, but I've not experienced it before. Take my word for it, it's not pretty. You try to think respectfully of your beloved but you hate her for leaving you.

> This emptiness gnaws at me;
> There's not enough whisky,
> And not enough food to fill
> The void you've left behind.
>
> You're no use to me, not here,
> Dead and gone! Yes, I love you.
> That's not the sodding point.
> Where are you Saint Seeley?
>
> You've nothing to worry about,
> You're a fucking icon. I've tried
> To be gracious, loving and kind
> But it's hard work, *entre-nous*.

So, fuck holidays. Fuck France.
Fuck the fucking-camper-van.
I've had enough of making do.
You fucked off. So...fuck you.

COMPLET
17 AUGUST 2015

On Saturday I went to La Crêperie Quartier d'été in La Forêt-Fouesnant for lunch. It was another place that we'd visited together on our trip, and I had traced its location from one of our holiday snaps. I didn't actually get lunch because it was full.

"Pardon, nous sommes complet," said the patron.

I reserved a table for dinner at 7.30pm instead and drove off to find somewhere to walk with Ted, and for me to have a cup of tea and read. We ended up by the ruins of the Abbaye Saint Maurice, next to a large wooded lake, and let the afternoon drift by until it was time to eat.

Seated on the terrace at 7.25pm, I ordered a small carafe of house white and six oysters. To say that they were exquisite would be doing them an injustice. They were *merveilleux*.

For the main course I had a buckwheat galette with scallops in a white sauce involving lambig (a Breton liqueur distilled from local rough cider) and, for dessert, a sweet crêpe with apple and caramel sauce, followed by a large espresso.

I know Chris would have relished every mouthful because for each course I chose exactly the same items that we had enjoyed together. The meal was a sort of gastronomic homage to our shared love of good food and the delights of travelling in France.

Afterwards, I spoke to the patron in broken French and told him about the visit Chris and I had made before and how much it meant to me to be back there, now that she had died. I tried to explain how the evening had been *parfait* but that without her nothing was *complet*.

He seemed to understand.

TREFEUNTEC
18 AUGUST 2015

It turned out that I was wrong about the hotel with a jacuzzi in Douarnenez. The website for Hotel Le Bretagne had looked spot-on, but when I got there it wasn't what I'd been expecting.

Wrong jacuzzi. Wrong hotel. Wrong town, in fact.

I took Ted out for a bad-tempered walk round the port looking for a restaurant for dinner later, found nothing that appealed to me, and got back to the hotel just in time for the jacuzzi I'd booked at 7.00pm. By this time, I'd decided that everything about Douarnenez, Brittany, France, holidays in general, and this one in particular, was crap.

But after 45 minutes in the jacuzzi I realised that my determination to repeat a past experience had come very close to robbing the present moment of any pleasure. I had a choice: to enjoy the evening as best as I could or to wallow in my disappointment that things hadn't gone according to plan.

The hotel receptionist booked me a table on the terrace of a good sea-front restaurant. I watched the sun go down over the harbour and ate well. Ted and I made our way back up the dark cobbled streets to the hotel and slept until late.

After breakfast, I set myself the task of having a good day somewhere that I knew Chris and I had not been; to enjoy the warmth of the sun and the feel of the breeze on my face; to be present to the moment as far as I could.

I didn't manage a whole day or even half a day without getting caught up in nostalgia and longing, but I did have one glorious hour without a care in the world, sitting on the headland at Trefeuntec, with Ted at my feet, and a Breton mermaid story to read.

BONNE ANNIVERSAIRE
21 AUGUST 2015

It is Chris's 49th birthday: the first one since she died. I bought a bottle of Clos du Papillon, our favourite white wine, to drink at 7.00pm when I knew that friends around the world would also be raising a glass to her memory.

Chris loved birthdays. Christmas was my thing but birthdays were hers. Not just a day but sometimes a whole week was dedicated to celebrating the wonder of having being born. As I waited for the appointed time, I reminisced silently with her about past birthdays.

Do you remember how we went to Demuth's last year for your birthday, and sat at the same table we had when we went there for our first date? The year before, we were in Portugal on holiday and we cooked dinner for our neighbours. In 2012, we invited some friends to join us round the campfire at Thistledown. In 2011, we went to Giffords Circus for the show and dinner afterwards. In 2010, we stayed in Long Island with Karen and Dick after our trip to Minnesota with the black bears. Every year was as special as we could make it.

This year, I've brought your photograph with me to Trefeuntec, in Finistère – World's End – on a headland I discovered last week. The side door of the camper van is open towards the Baie de Douarnenez; Ted is cooling off in the shade after scoffing his birthday dinner (I put some tuna on his biscuits); it is silent apart from the sound of waves lapping the rocks; the sun has some way to go before it sets over the far horizon, but the shadows are already long and the birds are coming home to roost. You'd like it here.

At 7.00pm precisely, I raised my glass towards her photograph.

Happy birthday my love, wherever you are.

SUNDAY SUNDAY
23 AUGUST 2015

On Sunday morning I woke at 8.30. I made my way to the washroom, dressed, took Ted for a quick functional walk, folded the bed away, sat down, put the kettle on for tea, and waited for it to boil. It was two days since Chris's birthday. I'd found it unexpectedly uplifting but I'd come down with a mighty thump. Another solitary day stretched out in front of me and I thought, what's the bloody point? I used to believe that I'd do rather well as a castaway. I quite like my own company and, as an introvert, most of the time what goes on inside my head is much more interesting to me than what goes on outside. Being on my own shouldn't really be a problem, should it? Chris of course was the complete opposite: an extrovert who found her identity in relationship with others.

It's a cliché that opposites attract, which is probably why we fitted together so well. Opposites also drive each other crazy. I'd sit quietly enjoying a rare moment of silence and she'd say, "What's the matter?" She'd come home from meeting yet another new group of fascinating people and tell me at length what one person I'd never met said to another person I'd never met, and my eyes would glaze over.

I'd give anything for the chance to piss each other off again.

9.5
24 AUGUST 2015

A few days later, it was exactly two years since Chris had her first seizure. All day long, I thought back to that night on holiday in Portugal. We were both asleep when the seizure began. I was woken up by the bed shaking. At first, I thought it was an earthquake. But she was having a full-blown clonic tonic fit: she was unconscious;

her body was rigid; she had violent spasms; she'd bitten her tongue and was breathing with difficulty.

It took about an hour from when I discovered what was really going on until the time she came to and we could get her in an ambulance. I called her name over and over again as I held her against me, trying to make sure she didn't choke.

Help arrived, first in the shape of a wonderful Icelandic nurse called Hjördis who was staying nearby, and then in the form of the paramedics who bundled us both into an ambulance and drove over the mountains to the nearest hospital. The hillsides were aflame with high-summer forest fires. It was like a scene from a Hollywood disaster movie.

Medication controlled her seizures and we had a year symptom-free before new tumours began to cause problems. Before another six months had passed, Chris died. I had thought she was going to die when she'd had the seizure in Portugal. I learned subsequently that she might have done, had her will to live not been so strong. Every day we had together after that night was a gift.

The image of an earthquake stayed with me and I wrote a poem as a way of saying thank you to Chris, for coming back from whatever unknowable place she went to when the seizure took her, and for giving us the time to learn to love each other properly. I called it "9·5" because that is the highest rating on the Richter scale of any recorded earthquake.

> We went about our lives
> as though immune from the shifting
> of the continents, unaffected
> by the mountains growing inch by inch,
> and the abyss that deepened daily
> under our feet.
>
> We didn't see it coming –
> the earthquake that shook our world.
> The flickering of the seismograph
> went unseen; the tectonic plates
> inside your head buckled
> and strained invisibly.

Until the fault-line slipped,
like San Andreas, collapsing
California into the midnight sea.

I thought you'd never come back.
But you weren't ready to leave.

You pulled yourself up from the depths
into my outstretched arms,
like the survivor of a great tsunami
and promised you'd stay
for the rest of your life.

You kept your word
my blue-eyed girl,
you snatched a glorious year
from that dark ocean
so we could learn to love
and be loved
in return.

Lost and Found

26 August 2015

Sometimes tiny happenstances trigger reflections and the urge to write. One night I lost my reading glasses. I felt for them in my top pocket and they weren't there. I looked around the camper van – it really isn't that big – and they were nowhere to be seen. It was nearly midnight and almost pitch black outside. I'd taken Ted for a walk just before. Maybe I'd dropped them somewhere on the campsite?

I was desperate to find them. The inconvenience I could manage, but Chris and I had chosen them together at Morgenthal Frederics while on holiday in New York in 2010 and their sentimental value far outweighed their purchase price. I quite often misplace things these days but this was serious. I began to berate myself for my stupidity: fancy putting them loose in my shirt pocket!

As best as I could, I retraced Ted's walk using the torch on my iPhone to search likely places, but to no avail. I went back to the camper van and checked inside again. Not a sign. I found my big torch and swept the ground nearby. Suddenly I saw a glint in the shadows. There they were, lying in the grass a couple of metres from the van, on a well-trodden route. I picked them up and looked at them in the torchlight. They were undamaged. Phew!

How is it that we can become so careless about things (and people) that are precious to us, when the novelty wears off? Maybe we have to lose them before we realise how much they really mean to us. Chris and I were lucky: we came close to losing each other a couple of times during our relationship but in the end we found in each other the person we wanted to spend the rest of our lives with. She taught me that love is a verb, not just a feeling. Choosing to love her has given my life meaning and dignity and I shall love her until the end of my days.

I WANNA HOLD YOUR HAND
28 AUGUST 2015

My daughter Georgie had given me the password to access her Netflix account so I could watch movies while I was away. One of them was a sci-fi pot-boiler called *Mission to Mars*. When the human protagonists meet the alien who is waiting to greet them (it's so predictable that it's not worth a spoiler alert) they entwine various numbers of digits and hold hands.

I wept.

OK, I'm a sucker for sentiment but I wept because it made me think what a fundamental and profoundly intimate gesture of connection it is to hold hands and, more immediately, how much I missed holding hands with Chris.

I say holding hands with Chris rather than holding Chris's hand, because of the essential mutuality of the act. I spoke recently with a widowed friend on the phone about what we miss most. There were many things.

"What about sex?" she asked.

"Yes, but even more than that," I said, "I miss not being able to walk down the street holding hands, feeling completely connected."

Chris and I had our own way of holding hands (I imagine every couple does). My right hand and her left hand came together in a way that I realise I cannot describe. It amused us that it had to be just so. Occasionally we'd tease each other by coming into dock with a digit misplaced. It would evoke a shriek of horrified laughter and the other would retract their hand, refusing to attempt to dock again until the whole hand was offered in the proper manner.

I've tried to reproduce the action in my mind but it's as though the memory is carried in my body. What's more, the memory can only be activated by our hands actually coming together. In the absence of Chris's hand, my hand doesn't know what to do.

THE GUEST HOUSE
31 AUGUST 2015

Ted and I return home tomorrow after five weeks. There's been some stormy weather on this trip, both literally (the rain is drumming on the roof of the camper van right now) and emotionally.

I had a hunch, earlier in the year, that the busyness of everyday life was beginning to get in the way of the real business of living. I came to France because, following Chris's death, I needed to make space to discover what I was avoiding and to experience whatever feelings came up.

What came up was just about everything: loneliness, yearning, joy, contentment, sorrow, pleasure, confusion, rage, despair, self-loathing and love. Nothing new there, you might say. Maybe so, but the difference is that I have been forced by the solitude of my "retreat" to face them without distraction or self-censorship. The experience reminds me of that wonderful Rumi poem, "The Guest House," in which he likens being human to a guest house and exhorts us to entertain all our feelings, even if they are "a crowd of sorrows," as welcome guests.

Of course, I'm not an enlightened being like Rumi and it has been very tough at times, though I've found writing a great solace and a way of keeping things moving, and getting out of a hole when I've fallen in. While I've been away I've written two new stories, a dozen blogs, a handful of poems and a long love letter to Chris.

A decade before, Chris had written an account of falling in love with me, which I'd always treasured and brought with me to France. When I re-read it, I felt that the honesty and vulnerability of her account demanded an equally frank response. So, I sat in the sunshine with Ted at my side and wrote the reciprocal story from my point of view. I wrote it for Chris, to commit to the page the truth of my very different journey to loving her and it's not for sharing here.

Writing it brought me very close to her and seemed to bring something about our relationship full-circle in a way that was deeply satisfying. Ours was no fairy-tale romance, but – as the letters showed – our love was deep and true. I realise once again that writing helps me find meaning and a sense of purpose, without which I could easily slip into anomie and depression. In the shifting landscape of my identity, "writer" has become figural, just as Chris hoped.

THE EAGLE HAS LANDED
9 SEPTEMBER 2015

Coming back to the hurly-burly of everyday life was never going to be easy. Ted and I got off the ferry in Portsmouth late on 2 September and made it back to Folly Cottage in the early hours of the morning. I unpacked a few essentials from the camper van and crawled into bed at about 2.00am for a few hours' sleep before plunging straight into the craziness of work the next day.

On Wednesday afternoon, I took Ted to stay at Hydegate Kennels (his look of reproach still haunts me) and travelled up to the National Exhibition Centre in Birmingham, where I had been asked to run some storytelling sessions for five hundred people at a two-day-long corporate event.

On the way back from Birmingham, I collected Ted and picked up an Australian friend from the railway station to stay for the weekend. On Monday we had an early start and a long drive to get to Ashridge to examine a doctoral thesis. The next day my guest left for London and a few hours later two other friends arrived for supper.

After the tranquillity of a five-week sojourn in rural France, this whirlwind of activity was an extraordinary contrast. Much as I enjoyed the work and the company of friends, I missed the simple daily routines of life in the bounded world of the camper van, and the time to reflect, write and be with my thoughts and feelings.

There is nowhere else I have to be today and I'm back at Folly Cottage, lying in bed in the Shepherd Hut with the door open, looking out onto the garden which has become lush and overgrown during the summer, thinking how much Chris would have loved the view. The rowan tree she planted is bursting with new pink berries; a wood-pigeon is clapping its wings and cooing from the rooftop of the house she lived in for 20 years; and Ted is stretched out beside me, waiting for me to get up and take him for a walk.

Finally we're home.

CHAPTER 7

AFTER ITHAKA

Over the next few months, I struggled to contain conflicting emotions. Chris's absence bore down on me heavily, yet I was also reawakening to *eros*. During the celebration at Matara, I had experienced the quickening embrace of a beautiful woman. I had needed to escape for a while so I went to the empty meditation room, shut the door and slept for an hour on the floor. As I was waking, a woman friend, whom both Chris and I had known for many years, quietly entered the room. Wordlessly, she lay down and wrapped her arms around me. As she held me, I felt a surge of erotic energy returning to my body. I yearned for Chris and at the same time I began to dream of the possibility of a new life for myself. It's apparent from my writing at the time that my grief became both sharper and more confused.

I wrote prolifically during this period, blogging several times a week, and was increasingly drawn to writing poetry as a way of expressing my feelings and trying to make sense of them. The effect of my friend's chaste embrace stayed with me, and I wrote a poem of gratitude for her:

Until you lay down by my side,
I was a seed locked in the dark,
held fast in cold, winter soil,
waiting, waiting, waiting...

Until you found me sleeping;
lent me the swell of your hips
and your breast for my head,
the life inside me was frozen.

This is how Aphrodite heals:
with the wisdom of her body.
Now it's stirring in my belly,
and I'm hungry for the light.

AFTER ITHAKA
10 SEPTEMBER 2015

Homer's *Odyssey*, that epic story of a man finding his way home in mid-life, ends with the hero's return to Ithaka, where he is finally reunited with his wife Penelope. We are left to wonder what happens next: do they grow old together; do they rule the kingdom wisely; does he resume his adventurous wandering?

It's such a compelling story that it's hard not to speculate. Many writers have: Nikos Kazantsakis wrote a famous modern sequel (substantially longer than the original poem) in which Odysseus, bored with family life, travels the world and eventually dies in Antarctica having spent time with Buddha, Jesus and Don Quixote; Tennyson's Ulysses rails against old age and calls his old comrades to journey with him once more: *to strive, to seek, to find, and not to yield*; Helen Luke, as an antidote to all this continued heroic striving, wrote a brilliant essay in which she imagined Odysseus maturing into old age alongside his queen.

But none, so far as I know, have contemplated the possibility of Penelope dying young and leaving Odysseus alone and heartbroken. When Chris and I found each other (I don't mean when we met but when, after a decade of struggle, we both decided to love each other at the same time) I knew that I had reached my Ithaka and that she was my Penelope. But it was not to last. My own personal narrative was naturally leading me to the question, "What happens after *my* Ithaka?"

Yesterday morning, I woke early with the urge to write a poem to seek an answer. I had a hunch that a formal poetic structure would help me to explore whatever images arose so I decided to try a similar verse form to the one used by Tennyson who wrote his poem "Ulysses" in unrhymed iambic pentameters.

The island that he fought so hard to reach
Has sunk beneath the waves and gone from sight.
T'was only ever She who made it real.
A king's no king without a queen to rule
The kingdom of his heart. There is no throne,

No palace to adorn, no marriage bed,
No place to lay his grey and weary head,
No song, no wine, no stories and no dance.
An old man widowed by a vengeful god,
There's nothing left of what he held so dear.

And so perforce, he finds himself at sea,
A shattered hulk beneath a starless sky,
A man without a mistress or a home.
The waves are still, the sirens do not call,
His grieving soul has lost the urge to roam.

Yet some faint hope is carried on the breeze:
The promise of a strange and distant land;
The perfume of a princess or a muse;
The whisper of a goddess in his ear;
The very breath of life upon his face.

PENNY PLAIN
14 SEPTEMBER 2015

No Ted for a week while I travel to Scotland and back to Ashridge for work. He's staying with Carole and David and I know he'll be happy there. Even so, I can't wait to see him next Saturday. We got so close while we were on holiday that I talk to him constantly, providing his answers myself if he doesn't respond. In Ted's absence, I miss Chris even more than usual and I lay in bed this morning wishing I could speak with her, feeling very sorry for myself.

Joan Didion wrote in *The Year of Magical Thinking* that for a long time after her husband died, she unconsciously acted as if he had just stepped outside and would return at any moment. She didn't get rid of his shoes, for example, because she knew deep down that "he would need them."

Anyone who has lost a loved one will understand how long it takes for the reality of their absence to sink in. I know Chris has died and that she's not coming back. It's just that I sometimes forget that she's not here. I turn my head to talk to her (always over my left shoulder for some reason) and often I've spoken a couple of sentences before I pull myself up short.

On holiday I realised the futility of these one-way conversations, so I wrote her a love letter instead. The French postal system was unable to guarantee delivery and I found my own way to share it with her. This morning, I wondered if a postcard would have been simpler: nothing fancy, just a Penny Plain.

If I could send a postcard
it wouldn't have a picture
of children eating ice-cream;
there'd be no saucy caption,
no view of Blackpool Tower.

I wouldn't write to tell you
that the weather here is bracing
or that we're having fun.
There'd be no newsy scribblings
scrawled upon the page.

No, the message I would send you
is simple and it's clear:
I don't know where you are, my love
but I wish that you were here.

NIGHT TRAIN
20 SEPTEMBER 2015

Last Tuesday, after a day's work in Scotland, I caught the overnight train to Euston. It was already past midnight when the Caledonian Sleeper pulled into Stirling. The attendant checked my name against the passenger list and welcomed me on board.

As the train pulled out of the station, I made my way to the passenger lounge and ordered a large whisky. I sat by the window sipping my solitary drink and looked out of the window, beyond my reflection, into the night. I slipped into a kind of reverie, thinking about how much Chris and I used to enjoy travelling on sleeper trains, especially on holiday.

Sometimes we would go down to Penzance from London on the Cornish Riviera Express for a long weekend; once we took our Morgan Roadster to the South of France on the SNCF Motorail. We loved the companionable intimacy of sharing a sleeping compartment, rattling through the countryside, stopping for mail in out-of-the-way stations in the middle of the night, bumping and clanking as the train divided or added more carriages en route.

We would reach across the gap to hold hands if we woke in the night and squeeze ourselves into a single bunk for a cuddle and snooze when the sun came up. Soon we'd hear a welcome knock on the door and the attendant would appear with early morning tea for us to drink in bed as we approached our destination, ready for a new adventure.

A sudden lurch as the train changed tracks brought me back to the present. I caught sight of my tired face in the window. I finished the whisky, went back to my compartment, climbed into the narrow bunk, wrapped myself in the duvet and lay awake most of the night, wishing Chris was there to share the journey.

PERCHANCE TO DREAM
23 SEPTEMBER 2015

Chris had the Shepherd Hut made about five years ago as a "room of her own." She decorated it exquisitely on the inside with a kind of post-modern, narrow-boat aesthetic, leaving the outside very plain to belie the cornucopia of delights within.

She loved to snooze in it on summer days and to light the stove and make tea in colder weather. Often, she would lie on the bed to read and sketch in her notebook. I didn't go in for months after she died but since getting back from holiday, when Ted and I spent five weeks cheek by jowl in the camper van, being in a house, even one as small as Folly Cottage, feels a bit strange so he and I sometimes spend a night in the hut.

> We go inside the Shepherd Hut;
> the stove is lit, the door is shut;
> we lie awake as darkness falls,
> our shadows dancing on the walls.
>
> Ted stretches out beside the fire;
> he lifts his head a little higher
> and looks at me as if to say:
> *She isn't here, she's gone away.*

I swallow hard and catch my breath.
What does he know of sudden death?
It's alright boy, she couldn't stay.
It's you and me. We'll be OK.

He settles down to sleep, and I,
I hug the blankets and I try
to conjure you from where you are:
my she-bear playing on a star.

Outside, the garden weeps with dew;
all living things are missing you.

GRIGNAN
2 OCTOBER 2015

Yesterday, I had a couple of hours en route to Lyon's St Exupery Airport to stop and draw breath as a frenetic month of travel and work drew to a close. I drove to Grignan, a gem of a Provençal country town that could have come straight out of a Peter Mayle novel. I parked the rented Polo in the cobbled main street and had a look round.

First, a Caveau des Vignerons to taste and buy a few bottles of local red wine. Then, I sat for half an hour reading my book and enjoying a café au lait in the main square, where I later had a delicious lunch of a goat cheese, sprout and spinach salad followed by freshly cooked tuna with polenta at the gloriously named Café Lulu Hazard.

Beside me, the bronze statue of Marie de Rabutin-Chantal, Marquise de Sévigné, after whom the square was named, glowed softly in the sunlight. How refreshing, I thought, to see the gentle, contemplative figure of a woman of letters celebrated at the heart of this community, instead of some fusty old general.

A few pedestrians wandered past my table but otherwise the square was tranquil. Until the town clock struck one (twice, for some arcane reason peculiar to French horology), disturbing a small flock of roosting pigeons who took it as their signal to flap across the square and take refuge on the opposing rooftops.

I needed only one more thing to confirm that I had found my way to heaven and there it was on the other side of the square:

Ma Main Amie, a tiny bookshop selling both second-hand books and exquisite new handmade editions of stories and poetry. I bought three slim volumes: a new letterpress pamphlet of Paul Celan's *Entretien dans le montagne* with uncut leaves; the *Elegies* of Anna Akhmatova in Russian and French; and a nice hardback reproduction of an eccentric 19th-century fairy tale by Alphonse Karr. They will take me ages to work through, dictionary in hand, but that's not the point. They are small treasures and I was very happy to give Mme Lefebvre, the owner of the shop, 35 euros for them.

Chris would have loved the town. But imagining her enjoyment only added to my delight. I felt joyful and alive and realised that I was there in my own right. I had stopped in Grignan to draw breath and found that I had literally begun to breathe more deeply.

NIGHT THOUGHTS
12 OCTOBER 2015

A week or so after getting home from Grignan I woke early in the morning, having imagined in the night that Chris was beside me. I missed her physical presence and it pained me to realise that we would never make love again. I turned on the light and began to write:

> My body stirs with memories of you
> and pleasures once upon a time we'd share:
> in spring-time rapture like the leaping hare
>
> and later under canvas, making love
> on summer nights when side by side we'd lie
> and chase the stars across the riven sky;
>
> or waking in the chilly light of dawn
> on autumn mornings half asleep in bed,
> and of two bodies making one instead.
>
> But now it's winter and you're not here.
> There is no comfort in your absent form;
> nowhere to shelter from the coming storm.

LITTORAL
22 OCTOBER 2015

Yesterday morning, having gone to bed late the night before, waking was a slow, dream-filled process. For an hour or more I drifted in and out of sleep, walking along the metaphorical shoreline that both divides and connects night and day.

The substance of my dreams sank back into my unconscious, leaving a single phrase echoing in my mind. The words seemed to have vital significance and even as I dreamt, I searched for a way to hold on to them.

What came to me was the image of taking home pebbles from the beach, each one chosen for its glistening beauty and vibrant colour. Usually, their allure evaporates along with the moistening seawater. Very occasionally however, we choose stones whose lustre survives dehydration undimmed. The words in the dream seemed to have this lustrous quality. As I sat up in bed, I spoke them aloud, content not to understand their meaning:

"The heart of acceptance is joy."

ONE YEAR ON
9 NOVEMBER 2015

This afternoon, I went to the Ai Weiwei exhibition at the Royal Academy. I booked the ticket a couple of weeks ago to coincide with a planned business trip to London. It only dawned on me a few days ago that it would be exactly one year since Chris and I went there to see the Anselm Kiefer exhibition on one of her last outings.

We'd driven up to Burlington House and parked in one of the blue badge spaces in the courtyard. A friend had travelled with us and we joined forces with another friend when we got there. Between us we managed the wheelchair quite comfortably. It was a great afternoon. Chris was on form and she absolutely loved the scale and boldness of Kiefer's work. Her eyes glittered with excitement and anticipation as we went from room to room. A month later she was dead.

It felt very strange to be there on my own today. I so wanted to talk to her about the exhibits. What would she have made of

Ai Weiwei's highly political art? Which piece would have drawn her most strongly? Perhaps, like me, it would have been *Straight*, an extraordinary sculpture made from 80 tons of reclaimed "rebar" steel reinforcing rods recovered from school buildings that collapsed in the 2008 Sichuan earthquake.

Thousands of children died in the earthquake, due to corrupt corner-cutting and shoddy construction. Each twisted reinforcing rod had been painstakingly straightened by hand in Weiwei's Beijing studio and assembled into a massive array on the gallery floor. I'm sure Chris would have been touched by the deep humanity and political intelligence underlying the form of the sculpture.

I'm also sure she would have found much in common with Weiwei's views on living artfully: "I think my stance and my way of life is my most important art," he said. I wonder what art Chris would have gone on to make, had she lived longer?

As I travel back on the train tonight, I'm left with two images: one, from a year ago, is of Kiefer's huge lead "canvases" studded with diamonds; the other of Weiwei's twisted metal rods being hammered back into shape. Despite their sorrowful weight, both images seem to presage some sort of hope.

WINDS OF CHANGE
28 NOVEMBER 2015

I nearly called this blog "Sailing Blind" or "Lost at Sea" because those titles were more resonant with my mood when I started writing a poem yesterday. "How can I steer a true course when the compass of my heart is broken?" I thought. But something shifted in me as I dwelt with the images that arose: a fog bank; slack sails; the sorrowful sounds of gulls; and warning buoys.

During the day, I spent hours writing and re-writing the few lines of verse that follow. Gradually, I realised that I may be lost but that I'm getting ready for a change. The journey that Chris and I shared is over but my voyage is not yet done. In the midst of desolation, a sense of possibility is also arising.

In less than a fortnight it will be a year since Chris died. I'm coming to understand that while grief is not ruled by calendrical time, there is wisdom in the old practice of mourning for a year and a day. The decorated wooden panel she fashioned in the last few weeks of her life after the Mort Brod we once saw in St Magnus Cathedral still hangs in the window by the front door as a memento mori, but soon I will take it down.

Then perhaps, a fresh breeze will spring up, blow away the fog and fill my sails once more. If it does, I'll know where it's coming from. Chris lived her life as fully and joyfully as she could. She would expect nothing less from me and even now I can hear her egging me on. As I listen to her voice, my attention shifts from the past to the present and I sense that the winds of change are coming.

The world is shrouded in grey fog:
no line of sight; no landmarks
by which to set a course.
The only sounds are screeching gulls,
and the dismal clang-clang clang-clang
of a distant marker buoy.

The broken compass of my heart,
knowing it is useless now, calls out:
Whither shall I steer if not to you –
my beacon and my guiding star?
Look to what is truly yours, you say.
Find your own way to the furthest shore.

So, I'm waiting for the fog to lift
and a fresh wind to fill my sails;
for I have untrod islands to explore
and untold tales to tell;
a few more chapters yet to write
before my book of life is done.

CHAPTER 8

SASSY BEAR

I was talking on Skype to a student in India when I heard a persistent knock on the door of Folly Cottage. It was 3.00pm – near enough – on Thursday 19 November 2015, just two weeks short of a year since Chris died. I put the student on hold and swung open the top half of the stable door to see who was calling.

It was Geoffrey Higgins, the owner of the Matara Centre. "I've got some difficult news," he said. "You'd better brace yourself." I couldn't imagine what the news might be. I took a deep breath and waited for him to speak again.

"It's Chris's memorial. It's badly damaged, I'm afraid. A tree came down in the storm and smashed it."

"What storm?" I asked. "I've been away for a few days."

"Last weekend. Sunday night," he said.

"But I don't understand."

"A freak accident," he said. "You'd better come and see for yourself."

"I will," I said. "I'll come up before it gets dark. Thank you for coming to tell me. I've not been back long; it was lucky that I was in."

"I've called by two or three times a day since it happened," he said, turning to leave. "I wanted to tell you in person."

I went back to my Skype call feeling numb. The student was quite talkative so I put on a listening face as my mind raced. How could it have happened? The memorial was set beneath two sturdy yew trees. They wouldn't have come down, I was sure of it. Maybe a branch had fallen in high wind? How badly damaged could it be? It was a solid lump of stone, for goodness' sake. We staggered through the rest of the call as I tried, and mostly failed, to focus on the student's questions.

As soon as we finished, I threw on a jacket, clipped Ted to his lead and walked along the road to Matara. The fallen tree had been cleared away but the sight that greeted me was heartbreaking.

The head and right foreleg of the bear on top of Chris's memorial stone had been completely severed. I looked around for the culprit and found a bare tree stump about 15 metres away, sawn to the ground. The centre of the trunk was rotten and soft as a sponge. The bole must have snapped in the storm and somehow threaded its way through the surrounding trees to fall like an executioner's axe on the bear's neck. It was as though Chris herself had been wantonly decapitated.

The thought of it hit me like a kick to the stomach; I bent over double and howled. Ted tugged at his lead, frightened by the noise I was making. I stopped when I ran out of breath and dropped to my knees to soothe him. "Sorry," I said. "I'm so sorry." I didn't know if I was talking to Ted, to Chris, or to the bear. When I'd calmed down a bit, I moved closer to the memorial and ran my hands over the broken creature, trying to make sense of what had happened. If only I'd come to see you more often; if I'd kept you cleaner; if I hadn't gone away for the weekend; if, if, if.

I laid my cheek against the bear's flank and recalled its origins. Chris had designed the memorial herself and, a few weeks before she died, we commissioned an old school friend of hers, stonecarver Lucy Churchill, to make it from Portland stone. It had to be a bear, of course. Chris had been fascinated by bears since she was a child. In 2010, for her 44th birthday, we'd travelled to Minnesota together to spend time with wild black bears in the woods. I used to joke with her that she was half-bear, half-woman and I had bought her the carved Nanavut bear that Lucy had used as the model for the memorial.

I ran my hand over the sway of its rump and thought how similar it felt to the curve of Chris's hips. I understood how, as Lucy had worked on the carving, it had acquired the name Sassy Bear. I remembered how significant it had been for Chris to claim her identity as an artist by the wording on the plinth and how I had decided after she died to include her full name Christine rather than the androgonous Chris, by which she was universally known. It seemed important that strangers coming across the memorial would know that she was a woman and not assume that she was a male artist.

The statue had looked magnificent when we installed it in time for the celebration of Chris's life, and now it was a wreck. I went back to Folly Cottage, found a shoebox, returned to Sassy Bear as dusk fell, put the broken pieces in the box, and took them home with me so they wouldn't go astray.

That evening, I poured myself the first of several large whiskies and sat by the fire wondering what it all meant. The damage to the bear – a catastrophic head wound – was so reminiscent of Chris's brain tumour. Was it some kind of message? Was she trying to tell me something? Was I doing or not doing something of which she disapproved? I'd been missing her warm physical presence beside me in bed and had been fantasising about the possibility of one day finding someone else to love and hold. Was that wrong of me?

"Don't blame me," I shouted at her picture. "You're the one who left."

Rage and tears and magical thinking: I couldn't shake off the thought that somehow I had made it happen. I fell into bed and slept fitfully; pictures of the storm kept coming into my whisky-fuddled mind, images of the tree falling and smashing the stone bear and Chris's head at the same time. When I woke up, I wondered briefly if it had all been a bad dream, but there were the pieces in the shoebox beside the bed.

I knew that in reality I wasn't to blame for the damage, but I felt a generalised sense of guilt that I was still alive when Chris was dead. With breakfast and coffee inside me, and sober now, I decided that it had been a wake-up call. I'd been wrapped up in work and not paying sufficient attention to Chris's memory or to my feelings or my own health. The bear was broken but I wouldn't let the storm break me. I promised myself that I would put things right and not go back to sleep again.

That was when I recalled a conversation Chris and I had once, long before she became ill, about the Japanese art of *kintsugi*: mending rare and precious porcelain with a special resin mixed with powdered gold so that the repair itself added beauty to the original object. I remembered that I'd even written a blog about it. I looked it up and found that I'd written these prophetic words:

Broken hearts, broken dreams, and broken lives cannot be unbroken but perhaps they can become whole again – and even more beautiful than before.

I wondered if it would be possible to mend Sassy Bear using this technique, and sent a message to Lucy Churchill to tell her about the damage and to ask her if we could repair the statue this way. She replied the same day and put me in touch with a colleague of hers, Sarah Healey-Dilkes, a specialist restorer of sculpture at the Victoria and Albert Museum. Sarah thought it might be possible to use the *kintsugi* technique and promised to come and see me and the statue soon. I'd done what I could for the time being and now I felt the urge to write a poem to Chris and the bear.

> When the tree fell in the night,
> did your bear-heart tremble
> at its terrible declension?
>
> When it struck your broad neck,
> did you cry out in reproach
> at nature's sacrilege?
>
> Did the forest weep for sorrow
> as your magnificent head
> crashed to the floor?
>
> And what of those who love you,
> brought to disbelieving tears
> by your shattered limbs?
>
> We remember the old songster:
> there is a crack in everything,
> that's how the light gets in.
>
> So we will tend your wounds,
> and make you whole again
> with seams of gold.
>
> The beauty of brokenness
> is the only poetry
> I care for now.

It took months to complete the repair. Sarah Healey-Dilkes and I couldn't get our diaries together until January. She came and cleaned the statue and drilled the pieces ready to join them, then went back to her studio and experimented with different types of gold leaf. Bad weather intervened and other friends helped by making a wooden frame and canvas cover for the sculpture to let it dry out properly. In June 2016, Sassy Bear was finally restored, the pieces joined together with gold seams. She is as wonderful in her woundedness as Chris was during her illness. I feel much more settled now that the bear is whole once more. I will look after her very carefully this winter.

Although Chris had commissioned the memorial, she had left it to me to decide where it should be placed. Kingscote has a fine old church and cemetery but neither Chris nor I were church-goers. Besides which, I discovered that the Church of England closely restricts the imagery that is permitted on memorials: angels and Celtic crosses are fine but animals are apparently considered to be idolatrous. So the churchyard was out.

The garden at Folly Cottage was my next thought but it's tiny and a very private space. Since one of the main reasons for having the memorial was to make a public statement about Chris's life and identity as an artist, it needed to be somewhere that people might come across it by chance. It was William Ayot who came up with the answer: "What about Matara?" he asked.

Matara was perfect: its gardens were open to the public; celebrations of all kinds were held in its grounds; and, as William reminded me, it's where Chris and I got married. It had already crossed my mind but it felt like a lot to ask of the venue's owner. "Ask for what you want," William said. "He can always say no."

Buoyed up by William's encouragement, I called into Matara one morning to see Geoffrey Higgins. He sat me down with a cup of coffee.

"I've got a favour to ask you," I said nervously.

"The answer is yes," he said. "Now, what is it you want?"

I paused a moment to let the warmth and generosity of his response sink in.

"I was wondering if you'd consider letting me put Chris's memorial stone somewhere in the grounds?" I continued.

"Of course," he said. "Do you know where you want to put it?"

"I haven't got that far. What do you think?"

"You can have it anywhere you like. Why don't you wander round and find the right spot?"

Which is how Sassy Bear had ended up in the shade of a pair of yew trees in a wooded corner of the Meditation Garden at Matara. It hadn't occurred to me that a tree might fall on it, let alone that such an accident would disturb me so much. I'd tried so hard to do the right things but nature had shown me how little control we have over our lives.

Now that Sassy Bear has been mended, I've been thinking again about what meaning to ascribe to the incident. I've concluded that there's something about the painful loss of perfection that highlights the dangers of idealising Chris now that she's dead. The trouble with creating a flawless myth is that the real person disappears. Chris was not a saint: she could be judgmental, demanding and insecure as well as being loving, generous and brilliant. I loved the whole person when she was alive and I need to remember her that way.

CHAPTER 9

BEING AND BECOMING

Although I was offered bereavement counselling by the Cotswold Hospice and had received excellent one-to-one support from a psychologist in the oncology department at Cheltenham Hospital in the weeks immediately before Chris died, I decided that I would rather follow my own path. I have had several long-term psychotherapeutic relationships in the past and knew that I could access that kind of help very easily if I wanted it along the way. In recent years, I had also trained with Judith Hemming in a systemic, soul-focused, therapeutic practice called Moving Constellations.

I began to sense the need for help as the anniversary of Chris's death approached. For the first six months, until the celebration of her life at the end of June 2015, life was painful but at least I felt that I knew who I was. I had been Chris's husband and carer, and now I was her widower. My whole sense of identity had become attached to my relationship with Chris; but who was I (and who might I become) now that she was gone?

Over the next few months, these questions provoked powerful and conflicted feelings: the crippling ache of absence; the impossible longing for Chris to return; the desperate desire to fill the void; the glimmering hope that one day I might love again. All these yearnings swirled around like strong tides battling opposing winds, resulting in what sailors call "confused waters" which rock the boat in sudden and unpredictable ways. As I grieved for Chris, I was also subject to wild, lascivious fantasies and unrequited infatuations. I was drowning and grasping for straws. I felt myself torn between a lost past and an unattainable future. My sense of living in the present was disappearing fast.

By the end of 2015, I knew I needed help. Fortunately this coincided with the first of two workshops I'd booked with Judith Hemming, exploring what she and her colleague Jutta ten Herkel call the five realms of somatic, personal, inter-personal, archetypal and divine experience. On the first morning, Judith and Jutta marked five large concentric rings on the floor to denote the five realms, from somatic in the centre to the outermost realm of the divine (or source).

"Sit quietly for a moment," Judith instructed. "Write down a meaningful question about which you want to know more, and put the piece of paper close to your heart. When you are ready, walk between the realms, spend some time in each and see what arises. Do it in silence and trust your subtle, intuitive knowing."

My question came easily: "Who am I now?"

I wrote it down, tucked the piece of paper in my breast pocket, and began to move between the realms with as much mindful attention as I could muster. The slow meditative movement reminded me of how Chris and I had walked the labyrinth in Chartres Cathedral and how afterwards she had spent the rest of the day drawing one intersection of the path in minute detail.

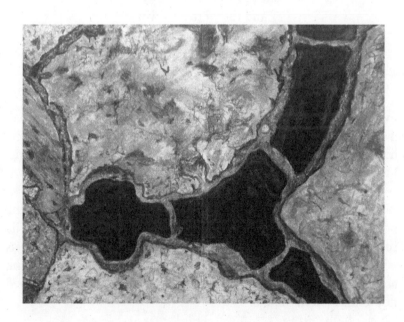

I tried to brush aside the inrush of thoughts and memories until I was aware of little except my breath, my heart beating, and the silent proximity of others in the room. What came in the end was a surprising and satisfying realisation that perhaps I was a verb rather than a noun: a being in the process of becoming.

Who am I now? I wanted to know.

So I followed the path
deeper and deeper into this world,
asking the question.

The ground under my feet offered no clues.
If the gods spoke, I didn't hear them.
The ancestors were all dumb.
My life made no sense.
My body mute.

None the wiser,
I retraced my steps,
spiralling outward to the Source,
and found each realm
silent as before.

Finally, I listened with my heart
and found the answer
already there:

Who am I now?

I am *returning.*

I was both returning to a sense of myself and, in common with all living things, I was also in the process of returning to the source, both metaphysically and literally. To be alive *is* to be returning, I thought.

And I am alive.

However, although I felt encouraged to be open to the possibility of new life and new love, I still found it hard to reconcile that desire with my love for Chris. Was I being unfaithful? Was even the thought of someone else a betrayal? What did Chris think about it all? It had been very hard when her memorial got smashed not to take it as a rebuke.

I took these questions to the second Five Realms workshop, just two days before the first anniversary of Chris's death. Judith offered me a constellation using the resources of the whole group to represent the many potential elements and people involved in the issue. Knowing Judith well and trusting her implicitly, I gratefully accepted. The constellation that followed was complex and moving and lasted for maybe an hour. I say maybe because it was so intense that it was hard to gauge the passing of time.

Members of the group volunteered to be representatives, their job being not to role-play but to trust the tacit wisdom of the whole field and to respond soulfully and intuitively to what unfolded. Judith set the constellation up with representatives for Chris; The Dead; Broken Memorial; Life; Friends; Death; Myths of Love; Christian Views on Loyalty; and New Woman. There were also a few other, less figural, roles which I'll omit at this stage for the sake of simplicity and clarity. Judith told most of the representatives to find their own places within the circle and then invited me to join the constellation.

As I stand up, Chris's representative comes straight over to me and throws her arms around my neck. It's as though Chris herself is holding me. I hug her back and we both sob for several minutes for the joy of our temporary reunion. Then Chris lets go of me and backs slowly away towards where Broken Memorial and The Dead are standing. I can't bear to see her go. It feels like losing her all over again.

As I stand rooted to the spot, the representative for Life turns and moves closer to Death, looking worried, with her hand over her mouth.

"I don't know what to do," I say.

"Just let go," Judith says.

I weep with my arms wrapped round my chest for comfort.

Judith invites the representatives for Friends and New Woman to join the constellation. Friends comes over to me and supports my weight from behind; I lean back into them. Chris has gone but I'm not alone.

New Woman walks over to where Life is standing. They hold each other while looking at me. I look back, fascinated but unable to take a step towards them. I'm not yet ready.

The representative for Chris's Broken Memorial, who has been looking away from me, turns and says, "Come and spend some time with me."

I walk forward and hold Broken Memorial in my arms, weeping. It's devastating to imagine the tree falling onto Sassy Bear during the storm and smashing her. As we rock back and forth, the representative for Life speaks to us: "I am Life and I can't tell the difference between you. I can't get closer at the moment but I'm watching out for you."

Life's intervention interrupts my tears.

"I'm sorry," I say to Broken Memorial.

"I need fixing," Broken Memorial replies.

Intuiting my sense of responsibility for what had happened to Sassy Bear, Judith instructs me, ironically, "Tell Broken Memorial 'It's my fault you got broken, even though it turns out I'm only human and it was a storm.'"

I can't bring myself to acknowledge that I haven't caused the damage, by omission if not by commission. Instead of following Judith's instruction, I tell Broken Memorial, "I should have been there."

Judith persists: "Tell Broken Memorial 'I've become a little inflated about my powers.'"

This time, I get it and relinquish the idea that it was my fault. I don't use Judith's words but say, "I couldn't have stopped it, but I wish I could have done. And I will fix you." The statement takes the charge out of the situation and I feel sad about the damage but no longer guilty because it happened. Now I turn and look in the direction of Life and New Woman who are still holding hands.

A representative for Christian Views on Loyalty, standing to one side, says to me, "Remember to be loyal to life and to love, just as your ancestors were. That's even bigger than this."

The representative for Friends, who has stayed close to my side since entering the constellation, says, "I have full love and support for you, Geoff. I want you to live your life with joy."

Loyalty responds, "When I hear that..."

Friends interrupts: "Whatever you do Geoff, our love remains."

I feel overwhelmed by the love and care of my real-world friends and sob, gasping for breath. The feeling is so strong that it's almost impossible to take in.

"Just breathe Geoff, and try to stay here," says Judith.

As my sobs subside, those representing The Dead speak: "We're here to take care of Chris. She's with us. She's the one I'm most committed to. I'm very touched with this sadness."

The Dead then speak directly to me: "Chris is safe with us until you come."

The representative for Chris speaks for the first time: "Now The Dead have said that, my consciousness is with them." And to me: "I need to go. I feel good now The Dead are here with me."

"Unclasp your arms and breathe," says Judith. "Did you hear what she said, Geoff?"

"Yes," I say to Chris, trembling with emotion. "I know you're in the right place but I don't want to let you go. I know The Dead will look after you."

The Dead speak again: "Remembering us is enough. To be remembered is beautiful. It means we can be here, with you."

Myths of Love moves to embrace Life and New Woman: "I am here in support of Life and you may join us." I look at the three of them standing together, smiling at me.

Life comes over and embraces me, saying, "It's nice to see you again."

The representative for Chris, standing with The Dead, calls over: "I feel good, very good. I feel like smiling."

I return Life's embrace, see Chris in the background smiling, and I laugh out loud.

"I like you," I tell Myths of Love. I look more closely at New Woman and feel my legs shaking. "I'm scared of you," I tell her.

New Woman says, "I have great respect for Chris. Whatever you give me you can never take away what you felt for Chris and you can take all the time you need. But I definitely fancy you."

Life, Myths of Love, New Woman and I stand in a circle, holding hands. Life is to my right, Myths of Love to my left and New Woman is opposite me.

A representative for Fate who has been standing outside the constellation as a witness, says, "It's as it should be." And one for Time, another witness, says, "Time is not neutral. Time is full of the joys and pains of life."

Judith asks me, "What's happening for you?"

"It feels good to be connected in this way to Life and Myths of Love," I say.

"And?" Judith queries.

"And New Woman," I reply. "And I need time."

Life interjects, "It's impossible to destroy what you had and that's not what I'm trying to do. I want you to have more."

Chris's representative nods vigorously in emphatic agreement.

Judith turns to the representative of Death: "How are you doing?"

"Generally I prefer a fight and he was making it too easy," says Death. "Now it's getting interesting."

Judith says to me, "You have to respond to Death because he's carrying something more. Let's imagine your soul has made some decisions about death, to do with the very early death of your father. True?"

"Yes," I reply.

"How is it for you, when you see Death not just as the passing of life but as something that has marked you all your life?" asks Judith.

Judith knows me and my history well and she has put her finger on a significant issue. Because my father was killed in a plane crash when I was very young, fear of death has marked my life since I was a small boy. In the constellation I realise that I have the chance to find a different way to relate to this archetypal force, one that enables me to stand up for myself in the face of the inevitable.

"I'm not giving up," I say to Death. He looks back, disdainful.

"I won't fight you but it's possible you have no place here," I try again, but I can see by the implacable look in his eye that Death is still not convinced.

"I won't fight you but you don't belong here yet," I say with more resolution. The words feel right. No-one can defeat death, but I can let him know that I believe it's not yet his time to claim me. Death's representative softens a little.

"I feel stronger," I tell Judith.

"What's it like feeling stronger?" she asks.

I'm flexing my knees and beginning to move: "There's more spring in my feet."

"So you have a bit of dance left in you," Judith concludes, laughing.

The constellation ends and we resume our seats. "I don't want us to talk about this just now, please. Whatever it is will find its place," Judith tells the room and we break for tea and coffee. I go outside to get some fresh air and feel full of love for Chris, hopeful for the future, and grateful for her encouragement to go on living and loving.

Three days later, we closed the workshop with a ritual acknowledging each of the five realms. A friend had given me a Jewish *yahrzeit* candle, with which to mark the anniversary of Chris's death. From its flame I lit a fresh wax taper to signify the gift she had given me during the constellation.

> Today I light a candle
> from the one I lit for you
> to mark the one-year passing
> of your passing into night.
>
> I wonder what the meaning is
> and suddenly I see
> you're trying hard to tell me that
> this candle burns for me.
>
> You're giving me your blessing
> to spark another flame
> and, knowing that I love you still,
> you bid me love again.
>
> I promise you I'll welcome love
> as long as I'm alive,
> for life and love are conjoined twins
> and both or neither thrive.
>
> The candle that I lit for you
> will always stay alight,
> but I will kindle this new fire
> and let myself burn bright.

It's difficult to convey the subtle and powerful movements that such rituals and constellations effect. We have little language, other than the lexicon of religion, to describe the workings of the soul. But I'm conscious that psychotherapy, as indicated by its etymological roots – *psyche therapeia* – has its origin in a more secular care of the soul. Bereavement affects our hearts and minds; our bodies and our souls. Its wounds go deep but not so deep that we cannot attempt to heal them through actively mourning our loss.

The constellation I've related did not magically stop me yearning for Chris, nor did I become immune to confusing platonic friendship with sexual attraction, but it did open the way to the possibility of new love. And I'd been right about needing time: it would be another six months before I was ready to meet someone whose love I could welcome and to whom I could open my heart. Both she and Chris feel very present as I write, and both are smiling.

CHAPTER 10

THE WIND RISES

The last time Chris and I went to the cinema was on 30 May 2014 to see *The Wind Rises*, the last great animé film Miyazaki directed at Studio Ghibli before he retired. A few days later a routine MRI scan revealed that Chris had new tumours and her health rapidly deteriorated.

Later I got the film on DVD and I've watched it several times since she died. The characters are far from heroic and their story is quietly underplayed. It's undoubtedly a masterpiece and about as far from a Hollywood blockbuster as you can get. Set in Japan in the 1930s, the story centres on a young aeronautical engineer and his struggle to create beautiful airplanes during turbulent, war-mongering times.

It's a tragic but ultimately uplifting tale. The clue is in the title which is taken from a famous poem by Paul Valéry, "Le Cimetière Marin," which is repeated several times by the young couple, whose love story the film chronicles, as a kind of touchstone for the times they live in and for their relationship. Valéry wrote the poem in 1920 in the immediate aftermath of the First World War: a visit to a seaside cemetery provokes a profound reflection on mortality, before the thrill of the salt-laden breeze and the crashing surf remind the poet of his own vitality and call him back to life. "The wind rises!" he writes. "We must try to live!"

Le vent se lève!...il faut tenter de vivre!

The phrase lodged in my mind when I first saw the film with Chris but its significance didn't really strike me until much later. It seems to characterise my experience during the first six months after the first anniversary of Chris's death, from the Five Realms workshop to the tentative beginnings of a new relationship. Looking back at what I wrote during that period, I can see that it includes a greater sense of hope and possibility alongside the raw pain of loss.

The door to new life and love had been unlocked by Chris's "blessing" during the constellation but it would be several months before it swung open. I continued to write blog posts and poems, as I travelled to Kenya, California, Mexico, New York and Ireland. Many of them are included in the next chapter, "Ashes to Ashes," about my long peregrination to scatter Chris's remains in places that were dear to us, but there are others to draw upon that reflect the messy, ongoing, everyday experience in the second year of my bereavement.

CHOOSING LIFE
6 DECEMBER 2015

Over the past few months, I've been in email contact with writer, storyteller and polymath Leslie van Gelder. She lost her husband to cancer in 2008 and generously got in touch to share some of her experience with grief. It wouldn't be appropriate to divulge our private correspondence, but I can say that I've found it enormously comforting to be reminded that although every grief is different, we don't have to navigate this territory alone.

What she writes on her website (www.leslievangelder.com) is in the public domain, and I want to recommend a piece called *Letters to a Young Widow* in which she writes to an imaginary, recently bereaved, friend. The fundamental question for the bereaved to address, she says, is as profound and simple as this:

Do I want to feel alive again or don't I?

In the numb aftershock of loss, the question doesn't even make sense. But she's right. It's taken me 12 months to realise that this is a real choice and that my answer (my deeply felt and embodied response) will determine every other choice I make.

Later in the same piece she speaks of well-meaning friends who – with misplaced sensitivity – would skate awkwardly over the surface of a conversation trying to avoid exacerbating her pain. It was a widowed friend of hers who knew exactly what to ask: "How are you getting by without touch? Have you found someone whose hand you can hold? Have you come to terms with the realisation that you are now no-one's 'first thought'?"

My answers to those same questions would be that I physically ache to touch and be touched, that I yearn to hold and be held, skin to skin; that I don't quite know how my hand would fit anyone else's; and that I've never felt more lonely in my life, despite the comfort of my children, Ted, and a multitude of loving friends.

But I do know that I want to feel alive again.

UNSEEN
20 DECEMBER 2015

When Chris was alive, I saw myself through her eyes. When we met, she was 34 and I was 51. We were together for 14 years and the difference in our ages was never an issue between us. I suppose the tacit logic of our relationship was that she would probably one day have to take care of me and that I would die first. In fact, our fates were the opposite of what we had imagined them to be.

Now she has gone, I see my reflection only in mirrors hanging on the wall. I expect to see myself as I was when she and I first met but, when I catch sight of my image, it's as though I'm meeting someone I haven't seen for a long time. I do a double take: is that really me?

The cognitive dissonance between the person I expect to see (the one with whom Chris fell in love) and the face in the mirror is shocking. I no longer know how the world sees me. Am I becoming invisible or am I still interesting and attractive and, if so, to whom?

I've known for a long time, because it's much talked about, that invisibility is an issue for some women as they age. I'd never thought about it in relation to men, and certainly not in relation to myself. Arrogance perhaps, or maybe just the natural consequence of being in a mutually loving relationship in which each is seen by the other.

I felt profoundly seen by Chris. She perceived my weaknesses and wounds, but she also saw through them to the best and most expansive part of me. That generous gaze was her great gift as a partner, friend and teacher. Apart from her physical presence, being seen in that way is what I miss most.

So maybe this is what I'm striving to understand: I haven't disappeared completely – I do good work in the world and have many friends – but in the absence of an intimate, loving gaze, I am learning what it is to be unseen. If I am not beloved, who am I? I look for glimpses of myself in the eyes of others but I'm realising that I have to find new ways to calibrate my sense of self.

Of course, my dog Ted thinks I'm brilliant.

But that's his job.

LOVE ACTUALLY
26 DECEMBER 2015

Chris and I would often watch *Love Actually* at Christmas. I thought I'd continue this tradition yesterday so, after lunch, I lit the fire and settled down with Ted, popped the DVD into the slot and clicked PLAY.

I suppose I should have anticipated the tsunami of tears that flowed over the next 90 minutes, but I didn't. Poor old Ted got so used to me bursting into sobs that after the first three or four times, instead of leaping onto my lap to sort me out, he stayed on the sofa across the room, briefly raised his head, opened one eye just to make sure I wasn't going to stop breathing, and went back to sleep.

It's easy to be sniffy about Richard Curtis films: middle-class characters (mostly white and mostly straight) falling in and out of love in posh surroundings. But, with a willing suspension of disbelief, both the beauty and pain of love are there to be relished. *Love Actually* has joy and passion and grief and loss in it, and love of many kinds from first love to last love; likely and unlikely couples are matched in requited and unrequited love. And not just romantic love: friendships, families and foolish fancies also have their place.

Chris especially liked the flawed Harry–Karen (Alan Rickman and Emma Thompson) pairing and Billy Mack's unlikely love for his manager Joe (Bill Nighy and Gregor Fisher). Over the years I've been touched by the plights of all of the film's lovestruck and lovelorn characters but yesterday, inevitably I suppose, I identified most strongly with the recently widowed Dan (Liam Neeson), both in his obvious love for his late wife and – I confess – in the fact that his misery diminishes somewhat when Claudia Schiffer takes a fancy to him.

Redux

15 January 2016

I woke up a few days ago with the word *redux* going through my mind. It's not a word I often use, though I was familiar with it from John Updike's *Rabbit Redux* and I had a vague idea of what it meant. It was such an odd word to be mulling on as I crossed over the threshold into consciousness that I decided to check the dictionary definition.

> adjective: **redux**
>
> 'riːdʌks/
> brought back; revived.
> past participle Latin *reducere* to bring back

I am reviving, I thought. I am coming back to life. There had been subtle changes in my body in the previous few weeks that seemed to signal such a revival. My hair, which had been dry and brittle for the past two and a half years, felt soft and silky and my fingernails had become stronger and stopped breaking.

"These are good signs," I said to myself. "I'm doing well."

But then I stopped to think about the word that had prompted this rather self-satisfied reflection. Redux: brought back. Brought back, not brought myself back. *Reducere* isn't a reflexive verb. I didn't do this to myself.

The truth is that I've been sustained by a filigree of love ever since Chris fell ill and especially since she died. So many friends – men and women – have held me in their thoughts; have written, emailed, called, skyped and visited; have offered convivial company; cooked for me; walked and talked with me; have witnessed my tears and held me in their arms; and have insisted that I have a place among the living. Without your loving kindness I would have disappeared.

Your love has brought me back to life. Thank you.

Red, White and Blue

4 February 2016

"Are they a gift? Would you like them wrapped?" asked the florist.

"A gift? Yes, I suppose so," I replied. "Wrapped would be nice, thank you."

One white rose and one red. I started buying roses like this a few months ago. It wasn't a conscious decision. Instead of walking past the flower shop, I stopped and went inside. The smell of the roses cut through the myriad other scents and demanded my attention.

A single bloom would be lonely, I reasoned. So, I bought two: a red one and a white one to keep it company. Not a whole bunch because then they'd get lost among the others. Even when it comes to roses, I'm an introvert.

I've been doing the same thing every couple of weeks since then. I choose them carefully: one red, one white, strong stemmed with unfurled petals. Open flowers that have lived a bit, not tight, mean, virginal buds. There's a pair of them in a vase on the kitchen table as I write these words. They are poignant yet comforting in their coupledom; ageing together side by side.

Chris loved having flowers in the house. I used to buy them for her. Now, I buy them for me.

They're still a gift.

ISLAND
9 MARCH 2016

Yesterday I came across a copy of José Saramago's delightful *Tale of the Unknown Island* on the office bookshelf. It's a parable, I suppose, about the journey a couple must make to find love. It was the inspiration for this melancholy poem about loving and losing Chris.

> We had searched our whole lives
> for that island that people call love,
> finding it, finally, in each other.
>
> I thought we'd stay there longer,
> that you would watch me grow old
> and I would be the first to leave.
>
> I'd write your name in many books
> and you'd paint mine, on the beach.
> Our story was meant to be that way.

But the gods of love decided otherwise.
It wasn't me but you who'd go before,
chosen first to seek the furthest shore.

I had to stay and watch you sail away.
Stay and learn to live once more alone,
reaping all that loving you has sown.

EXCEPT THOU BLESS ME
2 APRIL 2016

I recently came across an intriguing biblical phrase. Karen Blixen liked it so much that she quoted it twice in *Out of Africa*. It's from the story of Jacob wrestling with the angel (Genesis 32:26). It's near dawn, the angel has already dislocated Jacob's hip, but he won't let go until he receives a blessing:

I will not let thee go, except thou bless me.

I'm not a Christian and I'm certainly not a biblical scholar. But I am fascinated by the resonance of the magisterial language of the King James Version, and by the deep truth – secular as well as sacred – that those words convey about our need for a blessing in order to let go.

Blixen writes poignantly about saying farewell to her farm in Kenya; how she took her leave of the many people, places and animals that she loved, in a deeply considered and unhurried way. She did not shy away from the exquisite bitter-sweetness of each act of separation. In a moving passage she tells of putting Rouge, her favourite horse, on the train to his new home in Naivasha: "I stood in the van and felt, for the last time, his silky muzzle against my hands and face. I will not let thee go, Rouge, except thou bless me." I felt something similar, when I packed up Chris's paintings, art books, paints and art materials earlier this week, on Easter Monday.

It took me five hours to sort through everything, to decide what few bits and pieces I would keep, and then to fit the rest into the camper van so I could take it to Chris's niece in Manchester. I knew that Chris had wanted Rosie to have her art stuff and I was glad to honour her intention, though it was painful to see the drawers and bookshelves emptied of so many familiar artefacts.

In the end, Rosie's excited glee on receiving the materials, and knowing that she would use them for her own inspired artwork, became the blessing that made it possible for me to let them go with a joyful heart.

Finding new homes for Chris's clothes, books, pictures, teddy bears and other precious things; taking her ashes to places she loved; renovating and rearranging Folly Cottage; writing a memoir, poems and these blogs. They are all heartfelt gestures of farewell to my darling girl.

Thou hast blessed me and I let thee go.

MID-WINTER
20 MAY 2016

At the turn of the year, I began to think that the darkest days of my bereavement were behind me. I was feeling good and looking forward to the next chapter in my life, whatever that would be. Since then, I've experienced symptoms of delayed shock from the trauma of Chris's illness and death. My body is letting me know that far from being out of the woods, I'm still caught in a dense thicket of grief.

"It's early days," friends tell me. "What do you expect?"

They are right, of course. It's scarcely 18 months since Chris died and I'm learning that however consciously and creatively one mourns a loss, it takes a long time to adjust at a cellular level. As my heart and soul struggle to rearrange themselves, my body signals their distress with a variety of uncomfortable symptoms.

The precise meaning of the message is hard to read but it is clear that I need to slow down a bit, work less and rest more. In mid-July I'll take up a two-week writing residency at Hawkwood College, Stroud. I've decided to use the time to see if I can shape the material from these blogs and other sources into a book. Maybe this process will help me slow down long enough to catch up with myself.

In the meantime, I need to remember that grief takes its own course and its own time. Perhaps it never ends, just changes character as the months and years pass. I've only been on this journey for a little over five hundred days, and right now, much as I long for spring, I have to accept that figuratively speaking, I'm somewhere in the middle of a long, dark winter.

Five hundred days
Since you left
My side.

Five hundred days
Yearning for light
To return.

Arctic bears hibernate
In the deep drifts
Of my heart,

Calling out your name
Again and again
In the dark.

Five hundred nights
Searching for you
In my dreams.

Five hundred more
Before the dawn
Of a new sun.

RANSOM
1 JUNE 2016

Chris took this picture of Kingscote Woods where she walked year-round for the two decades she lived in the nearby village. Ted and I still go there most days to stretch our legs and take in the sights and scents of this quintessential strip of Cotswold woodland. He loves to run free, chase pheasants and scrabble in the undergrowth while I tramp along the footpath, remembering Chris and our shared delight in knowing the seasonal cycles of this modest place so intimately.

In a quiet, understated way, the transience of life is very apparent here: flowers bloom and fade; new saplings reach for the light while old trees fall and rot; blackbirds and thrushes nest and fledge; a scattering of bones and fur marks the demise of some small creature. Life and death are intertwined, two sides of a single coin.

Novelist David Malouf puts this beautifully in *Ransom*, in which he reimagines the meeting between King Priam of Troy and Achilles, the Greek warrior who killed his son Hector. As in *The Iliad*, Priam enters the camp of his enemy to plead with Achilles for the return of Hector's body. The old man is wise in his understanding of the world and eloquent in his grief:

> We are mortals, not gods. We die. Death is in our nature. Without that fee paid in advance, the world does not come to us. That is the hard bargain that life makes with us – with all of us, every one – and the condition we share. And for that reason, if for no other, we should have pity for one another's losses. For the sorrows that must come sooner or later to each one of us, in a world we enter only on mortal terms.

For every living creature, life demands a ransom.

Chris has paid hers. Mine is to come.

I think of her and smile.

CHAPTER 11

ASHES TO ASHES

Not long after Chris was discharged from hospital to spend her last few weeks at home, she sat up in bed one morning, with something on her mind.

"What are you going to do with my ashes?" she asked.

"I don't know," I replied. "We haven't got a mantelpiece so that's out."

"Seriously," she said. "I'd like you to think about it."

"What do *you* want me to do?" I countered, playing for time.

"I can imagine you doing something like Martin Sheen did with his son's ashes in *The Way*," she replied. "Not the Camino maybe, but some kind of journey. It's up to you."

"OK," I said. "I'll have a think and we'll talk about it again."

We bought a vintage, hand-painted, tin trunk in which to keep her ashes until they were scattered, but I put off the conversation about when and where that would happen, until it was too late. In the end, I had to decide by myself what kind of journey it would be.

Rather than a pilgrimage (with its connotation of a single destination) I settled on the idea of a *peregrination*: a sacred wandering reminiscent of the old Celtic monks like St Brendan, who called themselves "peregrini" as they voyaged the western seas and made landfall on mythical islands. For them it was their experience of the journey that mattered most.

Inspired by this idea, I decided to spread Chris's ashes in some of our favourite places, where I could enjoy good memories and take my time to say farewell. First though, I had to collect her ashes from the undertakers. I hadn't ordered an urn, so they gave them to me in a polythene bag, sealed with a wire twist. I took them home, put the bag into the tin trunk, and slid it under the bed until my peregrination began. That evening, I recalled the brief conversation I'd had with the undertaker, and wrote:

> Today I hold the weight of you again.
> Your mortal remains, unscattered:
>
> Flecks of calcium and fine grey dust,
> Remnants of a life that mattered.
>
> *We leave as we arrive,*
> The undertaker claims,
>
> *A bag of ashes and a baby*
> *Weighing just the same.*
>
> Ashes to ashes,
> Earth to earth.
>
> The measure of our death
> It seems, identical to birth.

When a friend invited me to attend a gathering of storytellers in Crete, I knew where my journey with Chris's mortal remains would begin. I also knew that I wanted to write about the experience.

AGIOS PAVLOS
19 JULY 2015

This morning, I woke to the gentle shooshing sound of waves lapping the shore of the bay below my window. Leaning out over the terrace and looking up, I could just see the tiny whitewashed hut that is the church of Agios Pavlos on a ledge in the cliff-face and, beside it, the shadow of a cave.

Chris had slept in the cave a few times when she came to Agios Pavlos for the first time in 2000. Her relationship with Mike had ended and she and I hadn't yet got together though we knew each other as friends. She'd gone to take classes at the yoga centre there.

She'd told me proudly how she'd travelled to Crete with just a backpack containing a toothbrush, a change of clothes and a copy of *Women Who Run With the Wolves*. She'd arrived by ferry from Agia Galini and waded ashore, a latter-day Aphrodite. After she died, I saw that she had written in her journal that it was one of the few times in her life when, as an adult, she had felt utterly free.

I'd taken her back there a few years later as a 40th birthday present. She'd attended yoga classes each morning while I'd walked a couple of miles along the shoreline to Triopetra, and back, more arduously, on circuitous inland tracks. In the afternoons, we'd dozed and swum and in the evenings we'd haunted the bar and had dinner. It had been an idyllic time.

I ate breakfast in the café, then crossed the beach and climbed the low rocky headland opposite, which the locals call the Sleeping Dragon. I sat for a while looking out to sea and then I made my way along the ridge of a sand-dune to the church and the cave where I planned to scatter some of Chris's ashes.

There were wax tapers for visitors to use in the tiny church. I lit one and left it burning beside a photograph of Chris that I'd taken with me. Outside, in the cave, I found a sheltered spot overlooking the bay and mixed a few handfuls of Chris's ashes into the dusty soil. As I did so, I felt a sense of joy and a rising energy in my body that told me this had been the right place to start.

By this time it was mid-morning and the sun was blazing down. I retraced my path over the sand-dune and followed the familiar route along the shoreline to Triopetra. It was a tough walk back (though I was determined to manage it without stopping). A cold beer, a shower and a long siesta later, I sat in the shade remembering our time there together and wrote for a while.

At about 6.30pm, when it was cooler and there were fewer people about, I changed and went down the beach. The water felt silky smooth on my skin as I swam out over the rocky shallows to deeper water. The poem I'd written that afternoon had made it clear to me that this was where the remainder of the ashes I'd brought with me belonged. I unscrewed the top of the jar underwater and, through my goggles, watched the cloud of grey-white particles drift down and away on the current. The first stage of our journey was done.

I brought you here for your 40th birthday.
Do you remember? You were mad for the sea.
Swim, you said. *Swim with me.*

So we swam toward the horizon:
you with your easy freestyle; me
splashing awkwardly behind.

I'd always been happiest on dry land
but deep water was your element.
There's nothing to fear, you said.
I won't let you drown.

We swam on through the beckoning waves
until we reached the Sleeping Dragon;
while below us, turquoise turned to aquamarine
and shafts of sunlight dissolved into darkness.

And I was not afraid.

So that years later, when the dragon roared,
I took your hand in mine and said, *Let's jump.*
You looked to see if you could trust me;
Yes, you said, *let's do it.*

For twelve months we played at the water's edge;
swimming together, side-by-side,
till the riptide came for us,
as we knew it would.

You smiled as you slipped from my grasp,
then down you went – free diving
into the unplumbed depths,
leaving this life behind.

Now you're swimming in different seas,
and I am slowly heading back to shore.

La Luna nel Pozzo
26 October 2015

It was another three months before I was ready to continue the journey. In October I flew to Bari and caught a train to Ostuni in Puglia, to visit the theatre school run by our dear friends Robert McNeer and Pia Wachter, where Chris learned and taught clowning for many years. We'd often been there together to play and laugh. I went to join Robert, Pia and their daughter Angel to say goodbye to Chris the clown.

There's a wonderful stone amphitheatre in the grounds of the old house. Behind the open stage is a small self-set pine tree that, according to Robert, just appeared one day. We decided that it was the perfect spot for Chris: up-stage and centre, in full view of the audience. Pia and Angel watched as I dug a small pit under the tree and carefully decanted the ashes.

Robert poured libations of olive oil and wine on my hands as I mixed the ashes into the soil together with some olives, grapes and almonds grown in the garden. We topped it off with a red nose, back-filled the remaining soil and smoothed it over. Then we put on our hats and our own red noses and made our clown farewells.

We took some pictures and finally sat side by side under the pine tree, reading poems and other words we had written for Chris. This is my poem, written an hour or two before our little ritual. In the tradition of clowning that informed our training, a length of rope is used to denote the performance area.

> Farewell sweet clown, no longer bound.
> Some spirit plucked you from life's cage;
> you crossed the rope and left the stage.
>
> Red nose and hat you left behind
> but took your laughter and your tears,
> delighted grin, and madcap leers.
>
> Now we must learn to fool alone,
> for you have gone away betimes.
> No duos now. Just solo mimes.
>
> With angel wings you mirror-dance
> while we on Earth your praises sound:
> *You are the clowning and the clowned.*

Robert read a poem he'd written while walking the labyrinth at Matara during the celebration of Chris's life. Angel offered a beautiful piece she had written last year, when she'd heard that Chris was unconscious and moving towards death:

> When I knew she was in a coma, I dreamt about her waking up and she said hello to me. I said it's alright you can go, and you'll always be in my heart. And I hope I'll see you again in my dreams. That's how I remember Chris, always smiling, there when I need her.

In the evening, we drove out to a resort called Torre Canne to eat at Dal Moro, a fish restaurant on the coast. Chris and I had been there several times over the years. Sitting round the table, just a few yards from the sea, with Robert, Pia and Angel, enjoying a bottle of white wine and some locally caught sea bass, was exactly the right way to end the day.

How Chris would have loved it.

SAFARI
26 FEBRUARY 2016

Safari is the Swahili word for journey. Tomorrow, my journey with Chris's ashes continues as I fly to Kenya to spend a few days on safari with Basecamp Masai Mara. It's the same camp Chris stayed at in April 2012. She adored her time in this primal landscape and we always planned to go together. We didn't make it so I'm taking some of her ashes with me to fulfil our intention as far as I can.

I'll also be taking the doll that Chris made and decorated as part of the Blank Twins art project with her collaborators, Kathy Skerritt and James Aldridge. She bound grasses and leaves picked from the Masai Mara to make the skirt and wrote on it the names of the different animals she saw there. I have a strong sense that it needs to return to Africa with her ashes.

Even though I was working and couldn't be with Chris when she went, it was a good time for us. There was no sign of the illness that was to strike her down the following year and we were feeling particularly loving and close. She took many photographs including one, she told me, of a lone male lion "looking for his pride." I wrote this poem for her in reply.

Out on the Masai Mara, you told me
I saw a lone male looking for his pride.
And I began to wonder about this idea

That pride lies somewhere out there,
Waiting to be found in the long grass;
That one's pride can be lost or found;

That one must look for it in another.
It puzzled me for quite a long time –
Until I thought of you lying beside me

And how you turn your head to look,
How you burnish me with your gaze
Until I become the mate you deserve.

Then I understood the lion's search
And how the lioness makes him king
For *she* is his pride – as you are mine.

KARIBU
1 MARCH 2016

The flight in a 12-seater, single-engined plane from Wilson Airport, Nairobi to Olkiombo airstrip in the Masai Mara took 50 minutes. At the airstrip, half a dozen liveried safari vehicles were waiting to ferry guests from a succession of incoming flights to various lodges and camps. A slender figure in Masai costume walked over and introduced himself as Steve from Basecamp.

"Really?" I said. "My wife came here in 2012 and she told me about a wonderful day she had with a guide named Steve." I showed him a picture of Chris.

He flashed a brilliant smile. "I remember her," he said. "She has not come with you?"

"No," I said. "She died from a brain tumour a year ago. But we always talked of coming to the Masai Mara together. That's why I'm here."

"I am very sorry to hear that she has died," he said. "But you are most welcome. *Karibu*, as we say here: Welcome."

Steve drove slowly to Basecamp with many detours to see the teeming wildlife, from warthogs to elephants. We had a close encounter with a massive solitary tusker, and came across a cheetah eating a recent kill. Four other safari trucks soon pulled up alongside us to watch the feast. Steve told me that in high season it would have been a dozen or more. Which was when I realised that the Masai Mara had become something of a theme park, albeit on very a grand scale. But I'm not cavilling: without the revenue generated by nature tourism, there would be no economic reason for Kenyans to protect the habitat and thus enable the survival of this unique eco-system. It's more fragile than it once was, and it would no doubt be better off without any human presence at all, but it's still here and it's still wonderful.

KWAHERE
2 MARCH 2016

This afternoon, I asked Steve to help me choose an acacia tree out on the savannah, to leave some of Chris's ashes under. "Certainly," he said. "We will find one with a good view." I thought for a while that he might have forgotten as we then spent a couple of hours looking at lions, cheetahs, hippopotamus, and two enormous crocodiles basking on the river bank.

I needn't have worried because later on, as he drove the Landcruiser up a long shallow incline, he nodded at a lone tree ahead of us. "I was thinking this one might be good. Do you like it?" The tree was strong and tall; grassland stretched out for miles in every direction; at the bottom of the hill we had just come up was an area of scrub where lions took their ease. "It's perfect," I said.

Steve pulled the vehicle to a halt near the tree and scanned the area for potential danger. "You can get out," he said. I walked over to the tree and picked up an ancient, bleached wildebeest horn that was lying there and used it to loosen the soil surrounding the base of the tree.

I unscrewed the lid of the container I'd been using to carry Chris's ashes and emptied them onto the ground. I used my hands to mix them with the dry soil, taking pleasure in handling her mortal remains so intimately. Then I took her Blank Twins doll that I'd brought with me and tucked it into a crevice in the bole of the tree. I decided to leave it there, wondering who or what would see it next and what they might do with it. It seemed fitting to leave an artful curiosity as a marker.

I bowed my head to say goodbye to Chris the lover of the more-than-human world. Here, I thought, as her soul makes its own safari, her ashes could enjoy forever the peace of wild things, an experience that she longed for during her lifetime.

"Kwahere ya kuonana," I said in borrowed and mispronounced Swahili. "Goodbye. Until we meet again."

NYOTA

5 MARCH 2016

Yesterday, just when I thought the Masai Mara had given me all of its gifts, I saw the African night sky properly for the first time. Basecamp had been too wooded to have a clear view of the stars (*Nyota* in Swahili) and the first night at Eagle View was overcast. But last night the constellations and the Milky Way were crystal clear. Orion hung low overhead, the Pleiades glimmered like a handful of diamonds, and the Great Bear beckoned me homeward.

During the last few months of her life, Chris's sense of self expanded, from egoic to planetary, and from planetary to cosmic. She believed, as she died, that she was returning to the cosmos, both in a literal sense as the atoms of her body disassociated and in a more mystical sense as her spirit was set free.

I sat by the side of the open fire, tilted my head back and looked through the small pair of binoculars I'd been using all week to spot game. A billion more stars flickered into life, filling the void with light. As I looked up at the cosmos of which we are formed and to which she has returned, I laughed out loud for joy.

After I placed some of Chris's ashes under the acacia, I wrote a poem to say goodbye to the part of her that she expressed through her restless and adventurous travelling. There are a few references in the third stanza that might require some prior explanation.

The character Genly Ai appears in Ursula Le Guin's *Left Hand of Darkness*, a favourite science fiction novel of ours. The Hainish were an advanced interplanetary civilisation whose method of making contact with emerging cultures was to send a single unarmed envoy – the mobile – supported at a distance by one or more stabiles, who stayed on the Hainish home world.

This method, they found by experience, was much more likely to lead to a mutually respectful and productive relationship than a show of superior force, though it sometimes cost the life of the mobile. Writing this in post-colonial Africa made me wonder how things might have been different had European countries been as enlightened as the Hainish.

How you loved going places!
You'd circled the world many times
Long before we met.

Even when we lived together
It was hard to know where you'd be
From one day to the next.

If we'd been Hainish
I would have been the stabile
And you, a Genly Ai, the mobile one.

Now your body has come to rest,
I do for you what I think you'd want:
I spread your ashes round the globe.

I'm letting go of your mortal remains
And every time I say farewell,
I do not weep. I think of you and smile.

You have not gone, but gone before,
Finding, as you knew you would,
A whole new cosmos to explore.

CALIFORNIA DREAMIN'
4 JUNE 2016

Tomorrow I fly to California on the next stage of my peregrination with Chris's ashes. I'll be staying with friends in San Francisco and Sonoma and then making my way down the coast to Esalen, where she went sometimes to paint with her beloved teacher Leigh Hyams.

After that, I'll go to San Miguel de Allende in Mexico to visit the house owned by Leigh's daugher Gina Hyams, where we once spent a memorable month. Chris painted a dozen fabulous canvases and I wrote a substantial chunk of *Coming Home to Story*. Then it's on to New York and Long Island with our old friend Karen Karp.

The previous trips to Crete, Italy and Africa were all quite brief. Now I'm taking nearly three weeks in North America to say goodbye to Chris the intrepid traveller, ebullient companion and fearlessly creative artist. I'm fortunate to have the time and the means to devote to this long journey of farewell, spread over many months and several continents. Unlike many who have been bereaved, I don't have young children to look after. I'm self-employed and my work commitments are flexible. Travel is expensive but every time

I've visited a special place to return Chris's ashes to the earth it's been profoundly nourishing and I've felt that it was money well spent. I'm following my instincts and letting her go slowly and mindfully, at a pace my heart can just about cope with.

No revelations, no grand words,
nothing but the daily task
of living in the void.

The keen edge of loss has dulled
to life-denying numbness,
the ache of absence.

Brute grief prefers a ragged blade,
a rusty dagger not a sword,
to do its dirty work.

A blunt knife cuts just as deep;
serrated, bloody wounds
that never seem to heal.

The gods, jealous of human love,
send a purblind butcher
to hack off their due.

They laugh but they don't know
how small a price this is,
for loving you.

THE GRACE OF THE WORLD
9 JUNE 2016

Several years ago, our friend Garth Gilchrist took Chris for a day out among the enormous redwoods in Mendocino County, north of San Francisco. She loved them, of course. Today Garth and I retraced their journey looking for a suitable spot to receive some of her ashes.

We left the city early and stopped for breakfast in the community of Boonville before making our way to Hendy Woods State Park. By mid-morning, the sun had burned off the overhanging cloud and the sky was clear and bright blue. We parked the car and followed a footpath into the woods.

The giant trees gathered us into their thousand-year-old domain. The air was still and silent apart from the caw of a solitary raven. As we walked, we were both drawn to one particular dead tree. Its vast bole lay straight and true, undisturbed since the day it had come away at the roots and crashed to the ground. Now it rested gracefully among its living companions, lightly covered in a shroud of fallen leaves, returning to the earth.

I clambered up onto the trunk and very slowly walked along its whole length, 89 paces, from top to bottom. I lay down on my back for a few minutes, supported by the tree, gazed up at the sky through the leaf canopy far above and thought of Chris and her passionate concern for the planet. Here, in the words of Wendell Berry's poem "The Peace of Wild Things," she could truly rest in the grace of the world.

Garth and I explored the ground near the base of the tree and found a deep den-like hollow. At the far end, tucked right under the bole there was a hidden chamber lit by a single shaft of sunlight. It was obvious to us both that this was the place.

We crumbled some earth into my hat (the only container we had) and I mixed in several handfuls of the ashes I had brought with me. Then I tipped the contents gently into the sunlit chamber. We pinned a photograph of Chris near the entrance, decorated it with a sprig of leaves, and said farewell to our mighty, darling girl.

Because of the great age to which they live, the trees in Hendy Woods are called *Sequoia sempervirens* (meaning ever strong or ever living). The next day, I wrote a mournful poem protesting this appellation.

It's a lie of course

They might last a thousand years
but in the end, even the mighty Sequoias
unplug their roots and fall

Nothing lives for ever

When our borrowed time expires
we die – and thus repay the debt
that we incurred at birth

Except for love

Body and bark return to the soil
shape and substance disappear
all that's left is love

And stories

ESALEN

13 JUNE 2016

After the redwoods of Northern California, I drove down the Pacific Coast to Esalen. Chris's experiences at Esalen were the foundation of her self-belief as an artist and I went with our friend Chad Morse who used to be in charge of the gardens there. It took very little time to find the perfect place to scatter the ashes we'd brought with us.

Hot Springs Creek runs through Esalen along a steep-sided gully. Chris would come to this spot by the bridge sometimes to draw or to make her way under it to the meditation hut overhanging the stream. The entrance to the track is marked by a threshold with the mantra *Be Free* inscribed in the concrete lintel. Tibetan prayer flags fluttered in the breeze as Chad and I made our way to the water's edge and put several handfuls of Chris's ashes into the fast-running water.

It was thrilling to watch the current take them away downstream to the Pacific. Chris felt very present and I loved the idea of her spirit swimming freely in the deep currents of the ocean with the whales that patrol these coastal waters. Afterwards, I went to the circular meditation hut and sat in silence for 40 minutes, saying farewell to Chris the wild-woman artist.

Then I walked to the famous Esalen hot tubs perched on the cliff a few hundred yards away, stripped off, climbed into the slightly sulphurous water, and stared out to sea for a long time, imagining Chris's essence spreading to the horizon. Later, I met Chad for dinner at Nepenthe, a one-time hippy haunt and now fashionable restaurant where, according to Chris's great friend and fellow artist Kathy Skerritt, they had once "laughed [their] asses off while eating cheese and drinking wine."

Chad had organised a bed for me at a friend's place in part of Esalen nicknamed New Yurt City. I slept well and was up early for a 7.30am hot tub and massage before hitting the road for the spectacular drive down Highway One to Los Angeles Airport for my flight to Mexico.

DIA DE LOS MUERTOS
14 JUNE 2016

I'm staying in the house in San Miguel de Allende where Chris and I once spent the best part of a month together, working side by side. The house is called *Casa Duende*, which means House of Spirit.

Leigh Hyams' daughter Gina, who owns the house, graciously invited me to stay here again.

Looking around, I recalled the joyful, passionate and intense time Chris and I shared in this glorious house. She painted every day under Leigh Hyams' watchful eye and I wrote several chapters of my first book. It was such an enjoyable and productive experience that it came to symbolise for us the honouring of our creative lives as artist and writer.

We spent a month here long ago;
we came to paint and write.
You faced the canvas every day,
and I was erudite.

And after, in the borrowed bed,
I held you in my arms
and wondered at the flecks of paint
that graced your naked charms.

The colours were much brighter then:
El Corazon, aflame.
Together we made love and art
and found they were the same.

I knew, after Chris died, that I had to come back here to remind myself of that period and of the place that had so nurtured our creativity, and to leave some of her ashes here in the garden. This afternoon, before it rained, I found a quiet spot close to the studio in which Chris painted and, with as little disturbance of the soil as possible, I mixed a few handfuls of ash into the loam at the foot of a tree and replaced the large stone that had covered the spot.

I bought the little clay figure in the picture from a craft shop in town. Death is celebrated as part of life in Mexico and the dead are made welcome in our lives at all times, not just during the three-day festival of El Dia de los Muertos. After the brief ritual in the garden, I left the figurine in the house to commune on Chris's behalf with the spirit of Leigh who lived here and died three years ago.

Although this place has much to do with Chris the artist, today I chose to say farewell to Chris the enthusiastic enabler and supporter of other people's creativity. When we got married, her first vow to me was: *I will encourage, support and dare you in your creativity – so that you grow fully and magnificently into yourself. I'll be your best cheerleader.* She was, and she still is, the best supporter I've ever had.

In the evening I went to a rooftop restaurant for dinner, feeling weighed down by her loss and further depressed by the nightly downpour of the rainy season, which perfectly matched my mood.

I sit alone, drinking margaritas,
wrapped in a blanket to keep out the cold,
as dark clouds gather over San Miguel.

The bustling streets below are empty now;
turistas shelter from the coming storm
in heated restaurants and cosy bars.

A peal of thunder silences the bells
of La Parroquīa; the world stands still
as lightning arcs across the moonless sky.

Fat drops of water parachute to earth,
then harder, faster, bouncing off the ground,
a slick curtain of rain to hide my tears.

They're for the time we had together here.
I've had enough of crying on my own,
it pleases me to watch the city weep.

HORTON POINT
19 JUNE 2016

There are 122 steps leading down to the beach at Horton Point, Long Island. Over the years, Chris walked down them many times with our friend Karen Karp to swim together in Long Island Sound. Karen's home nearby was one of Chris's favourite hangouts and she went there whenever she could. We stayed there in August 2002, for our first holiday as a couple, and frequently returned.

Today Karen, Dick (her partner) and I took some of Chris's ashes to the shore. Karen and I waded out a few yards and I released a handful into the water. Karen stood nearby in her wetsuit. I passed her the container with the remaining ashes.

"Do you want to take our girl for a swim?" I asked.

Karen nodded, plunged into the sea and struck out towards the horizon. Soon she allowed the tide to catch her and drift her parallel to the shoreline. After ten minutes or so, she made her way back to where Dick and I were waiting and handed me the empty container.

"I opened the lid and let her ashes flow out as I went along," she said. "It was beautiful to swim with her again. Thank you."

As she spoke, a small white butterfly flitted around us. They are commonplace here but it was a delightful moment and lifted our spirits. Chris had a great gift for friendship and she would have been thrilled that two of our dearest friends were able to say farewell to her in this way with me.

As I write these words, Karen and Dick are cooking dinner and compiling the playlist for their wedding in New York on 1 July. They are getting married after 20 years together and I wouldn't miss it for the world. Chris, I'm sure, will be looking over our shoulders to witness them exchanging their vows in City Hall, and dancing with us at the celebration party afterwards. I'm not going to be giving a speech but if I was, I think I would say, from what Chris and I learned during our time together: life is short and precious; enjoy each other every moment you can; and love really is all you need.

A few days later, my North American journey was over. I flew back to England, picked up Ted from the dog-minders and began to think about the next stages of my peregrination. They would be much closer to home because I had already celebrated many far-flung dimensions of Chris's life and now it was time to focus on her family and the more personal aspects of our life together.

Pushing up Bramleys
9 July 2016

Chris loved apple pie. When friends asked her, during the last six months of her life, if there was anything they could do to help, she frequently asked them to make her an apple pie. Pies of all shapes and sizes were delivered to the house and to hospital wards. All were consumed with gusto and gratitude, and gouts of fresh cream.

Which is why, a year ago, Chris's sister Helen and their mum Joan chose to plant a Bramley, queen of cooking apples, in her memory, in a secluded orchard a few streets from Helen's house in Manchester.

I drove there today, with some of Chris's ashes, to stay with Helen and her children Adam (20) and Rosie (17) and to visit the tree. Joan couldn't get there because of a problem with her train but, after some to-ing and fro-ing, we decided to go ahead without her.

After lunch Helen, Rosie, Adam and I took Ted with us to the orchard. Helen pointed out the tree, its slender young branches already bearing fruit, and I dug a small hole close to the base but far enough away so as not to damage the roots. The four of us took it in turns to mix the ashes with the fine dark loam, then I re-filled the hole and tamped the soil down. Before leaving, we said a silent farewell to Chris: beloved daughter and sister; loving and generous aunt.

During her lifetime, Chris nourished the talents of all around her, from her artistic niece Rosie to her doctoral students, which made me think she would be pleased that her ashes will help the tree grow. In a year or two, with a bit of luck, it will produce enough plump Bramleys to make a good-sized apple pie. I've already put in my order for a big fat slice. With cream.

KILMURRY
10 AUGUST 2016

The picture overleaf is the Kilmurry beat on the River Blackwater near Fermoy, in Ireland. Chris and I came here ten years ago for a day's fishing with guide (and world champion fly-caster) Glenda Powell. We'd been to the Cape Clear Island Storytelling Festival and were coming to the end of a wonderful camping trip round Ireland. I treated her to the day as a late birthday present.

Today I came back to spend an afternoon fishing with Glenda and to put some of Chris's ashes in the river. In the course of four hours we covered a half mile of river and, with Glenda's expert guidance, I caught three beautiful small brown trout. I remember that Chris had caught a baby salmon on her second or third cast and crowed about it for weeks.

There were kingfishers on the river this afternoon; salmon breaking the surface mid-stream; an egret fishing in the margins; and mink scurrying around on the bank. Ted had the run of the place and was in and out of the water all afternoon. I don't believe in heaven but if I did, it would be like this: sunlight sparkling on a salmon run; trout lurking in the shallows; happy dog trotting nearby.

Glenda remembered Chris and we talked all afternoon about life, love and loss as we fly-fished our way slowly downstream. At about 6.00pm, we waded out into a fast-running stretch of water and emptied a small container of Chris's ashes into the river. Glenda said a prayer and I thanked Chris for all the wonderful adventures we had together, and for being my playmate as well as my soulmate.

Afterwards, we toasted her memory with a dram of Irish whiskey, and Glenda invited me to stay and camp by the river for the night instead of driving to a campsite. So, I'm writing this by the light of a coal fire in the wooden fisherman's hut by the riverbank.

I cooked some steak on the barbecue and had it for supper with a bottle of Guinness. Ted had a fresh marrow bone, also from the butcher in Fermoy, and we settled down by the fire to digest our meals like a couple of full-bellied hunter-gatherers.

It's 10.00pm now and dark outside. Soon Ted and I will hunker down for the night in Rosie the camper van. I plan to wake early, get in a couple of hours fishing before breakfast, and head to Rosslare for our final 24 hours before the ferry home on Friday evening.

DADDY'S GIRL
6 NOVEMBER 2016

I never met Chris's dad, Jim. He died when she was only 24, long before we got to know each other. Today, I drove with Ted to the crematorium where Jim's ashes had been scattered, to meet

Chris's sister Helen and her mum Joan. They had brought a spring-flowering plant and a trowel and I handed them a container of Chris's ashes for them to perform their own rite of farewell.

Ted and I waited in the car as they went off into a wooded area, beyond our sight. They'd asked for privacy and I understood that this time I needed to stand back and allow Chris's immediate family the opportunity to say goodbye in their own way. They returned half an hour later, chilled by the damp autumn weather but smiling.

"Did it go well?" I asked.

"Would you like to come and see?" replied Joan.

I followed them back up the path to a stand of silver birches.

"Look," said Joan. "This is the same place we scattered her dad's ashes."

"We put some underneath and scattered the rest," said Helen, pointing to the newly planted *Osmanthus burkwoodii*. It took a bit of doing I can tell you; the ground was as hard as a brick."

"And we put this up," said Joan, indicating a small brass plaque on a nearby tree, which read:

CHRIS

HERE WITH HER DAD

R.I.P.

After a little while we went to a local pub for Sunday lunch and then Helen left for Manchester and I drove Joan back to her home in Stratford-upon-Avon. As we made our way north, she turned to me in the late afternoon half-light and said quietly, "Chris loved her family – all of us. But she adored Jim. The two of them used to go skiing most years, you know. She was a daddy's girl, really. I'm very glad they are together again."

AMUSEZ-VOUS. MERDE!
29 NOVEMBER 2016

Chris loved her work at Schumacher College. She felt at home there: nourished, appreciated and given licence to work at the juicy edges of her practice as a facilitator and teacher. She adored the long walks along the River Dart that she took each year with her MSc students, so when I spoke recently with her dear friend and collaborator Toni Spencer, we decided to go there together to spend some time reminiscing and to put some of Chris's ashes in the river.

While Ted chewed fallen twigs and splashed in the water, Toni and I made a fire on the bank, drank from a thermos of tea, and talked about Chris and about what was happening in our own lives. I spoke about finding new love in the midst of grief and Toni told me about her own journey of transition.

Only then did I understand why I had been called so strongly to this place. It was time to say goodbye to the woman that Chris was becoming before she died: a woman claiming her power and place in the world; painting, drawing and clowning with great gusto; writing boldly and creatively; and bringing her unique practice of *artful inquiry* into being.

Toni and I took it in turns to step into the Dart and release Chris's ashes into the water. When I got back to shore, Toni pointed out a robin that had been dancing on my abandoned jacket while I was standing in the middle of the river. It reminded me of the robin that had made its way into Folly Cottage just after Chris died, but before I had a chance to get misty-eyed and sentimental, it defecated on a nearby stone and flew off.

"Amusez-vous. Merde!" clown teacher Philippe Gaulier would say to his students. Chris quoted it in her PhD thesis to stand for a "tenacious, non-sentimental insistence on life within loss that is honest, ready to risk failure, and absolutely courageous."

It's how Chris lived her life and it's how I'm trying to live mine.

THIS ROAD NOW IS ENDING
3 DECEMBER 2016

Over the last 18 months, I have scattered Chris's ashes in many parts of the world: Crete, Italy, Africa, the United States, Mexico, Ireland

and some special places in the UK. Today is the second anniversary of her death and time to complete my long peregrination by laying the last of her remains to rest in Kingscote, the village she called home for 20 years.

Friends come to call: Miche and Flora for breakfast; Ben Bennett, our ex-neighbour, for a cup of coffee; Carole and David for tea and cake. During the day, we visit Chris's memorial and peek under Sassy Bear's winter covers; mix some ashes into the earth beneath the stone Buddha in the garden at Folly Cottage; and place the remainder into the heart of a hollow tree in Kingscote Woods by the light of a crescent moon.

Among her ashes, deep in the soil, I bury a fire opal that I'd brought back specially from my trip to Mexico in June. It's said that the Romans believed opals to be the most precious of all gemstones because they contain the colours of all the others and that the Bedouin used to think that they contained lightning and fell from the sky during thunderstorms. I want Chris to have some of that opaline fire to keep her warm in the cold, cold earth.

As I say farewell to her material form for the last time, I feel a deep sense of peace and satisfaction. I remember a much-loved volume of poetry by Rolf Jacobsen called *The Roads Have Come to an End Now* and the thought comes into my mind with a smile that though this road now is ending, the journey of my life is not yet done. I write this poem to mark the end of my peregrination.

Like Brendan and his tonsured crew,
wandering the white-crested sea lanes
to the secret islands of the setting sun,
I traced the wild margins of the world.

Not a pilgrimage but a camino of sorts,
I followed the lonely path of mourning
strewing the ashes of my darling girl
to mark her journey through this life.

The healing that I sought, discovered
not in churches and their sacraments
but in the journey to far-flung places
and coming home to find myself anew.

CHAPTER 12

WRITTEN ON THE BODY

From the time of Chris's first seizure in Portugal, to her death 18 months later, and for nearly a year after that, my body seemed to run on automatic pilot. I felt surprisingly fit and well, although friends noticed how much weight I'd lost. Caring for Chris had exhausted me but somehow the mechanism of my body kept going. It was as though my heart and mind had raced ahead, trying to cope with the onslaught of grief, leaving my body behind to do its own thing.

In October 2015, my body finally caught up with me.

I'd been away on one of the first legs of my peregrination, in Southern Italy. After a late flight back, I climbed into bed at 3.00am. By the next morning, my joints ached, I had a headache and a raging sore throat, and a blood blister had sprung up on my lip. I dosed myself with Lemsip and echinacea. It was only a cold but I felt as though I'd suddenly run out of road, like the cartoon character Wile E. Coyote, improbably suspended in mid-air above the canyon until he looks down and gravity takes over.

I wrote a self-pitying, grumpy poem called "Grievous Bodily Harm" as I lay in bed but it didn't make me feel any better.

> This morning, I woke up
> frayed at the edges,
> feeling sorry for myself:
> grumbling joints,
> blood blister on lip,
> bellyache, sore head,
> incipient cold.

I'd been waiting for my body
to mirror the pain I feel,
the sense of loss, the void
where once you were,
the sheer, fucking,
what's-the-point-of-it-all.

Now it's finally happened,
I don't much care for it.

Will it be downhill now,
until I crumble into dust?
I never was any good
at looking after myself,
except as an object of desire.

Now that's gone too.

It would be nice to find
a happy twist to this poem,
a little upturn at the end.

But I can't.

I hoped that what I was experiencing would be just a temporary blip and that my good health would quickly return. But deep down, I sensed that it presaged something more serious and I was right. The cold ran its course but was followed by a tedious assortment of aches, pains and ailments that have persisted for months. I've had a wisdom tooth removed; discovered a benign cyst on a kidney and polyps in my gall bladder; experienced psoriasis for the first time in my life; and suffered the unwelcome indignity of cold sores and a loss of libido. As I write these words, I have an inflamed hip joint and sciatic pain.

As the symptoms, particularly of my psoriasis, worsened, I realised that the underlying causes of my condition were probably more than just a delayed physical abreaction to the trauma of Chris's illness and death. Jung argued that psychosomatic symptoms are messages from the unconscious and that we ignore them at our peril. What, I wondered, was my body trying to tell me?

I'm still wrestling with that question. I think that it has something to do with the puzzle of why Chris died and I'm still here.

I feel a vague but powerful sense of guilt. Why was she struck down and not me? Can I allow myself to accept that it wasn't my fault, that there was nothing I could have done to save her? Harder still, do I really believe that it's alright for me to love again, now that she has gone? I wrote a blog post recently, looking for some answers.

STIGMATA
1 MAY 2016

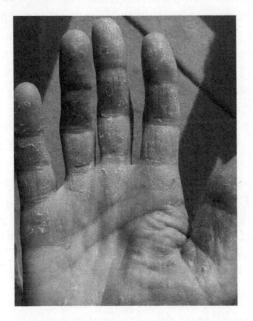

stigmata \stig-ˈmä-tə\ *plural* of ***stigma*** \stig-mə\

1. a scar left by a hot iron = brand (archaic)

2. a mark of shame or discredit

3. an identifying mark or characteristic

4. a specific diagnostic sign of a disease

In the past few weeks I've developed a condition called psoriasis, which both cracks the skin and covers it with unsightly blotches and callouses. It has particularly affected my hands and feet, which blistered yesterday for no reason while I was walking in Paris.

I hobbled the last mile from the Metro to the hotel and revived myself with a cold beer at the bar.

According to my homeopath (who is also a trained medical doctor), psoriasis is an auto-immune condition. In other words, you don't catch it from anyone, the body does it by itself. Her explanation was that my adrenal system had been working overtime ever since Chris had her fit in Portugal two and a half years ago.

Under certain conditions, adrenaline and cortisol override the underlying immune system of the body, the homeopath told me. In the short term, they boost energy, reduce our capacity to feel pain, and suppress the symptoms of minor illnesses; they enable extraordinary feats of strength and endurance for our immediate protection. But if we can't switch them off when they've done their job, they damage us.

"It's a bit like living on coffee and cake instead of a balanced diet," she said. "They give you a quick boost but in the long run they don't nourish you."

Later, I came across some research in the *British Medical Journal* that showed a disproportionately high level of mortality among the newly widowed. People do actually die of grief, it seems, and I wondered if a prolonged stress reaction might be a contributory factor. The same research showed that mortality rates return to normal after 6–12 months. Except, there is no normal any more.

As Joan Didion says in *The Year of Magical Thinking*:

Grief turns out to be a place none of us know until we reach it... Nor can we know ahead of the fact...the unending absence that follows, the void, the very opposite of meaning, the relentless succession of moments during which we will confront the experience of meaninglessness itself.

In the "unending absence" following Chris's death, grief has chosen this moment to inscribe itself on my body like a brand or tattoo. These stigmata are signs of my suffering; they are uncomfortable and unsightly but they are neither punitive nor shameful.

These aren't the marks of Christ upon my hands,
though it was a kind of crucifixion
to watch you – helpless – as you died.

You flayed me like the Lindworm's bride;
all seven of my skins you stripped away
then scrubbed my naked flesh with lye.

Alive, you would have bathed me in warm milk
and held me tightly in your loving arms
until I was myself again.

If you had lived, I would not still be raw
nor grief's astringent cover me with sores.
They are not Christ's – these marks – but yours.

At one level, I think the psoriasis is a wake-up call to look after myself properly: to allow grief to move through me; to change my diet and eat better; to exercise and get proper rest; and to focus my energy on what sparks joy and makes me content. It's absolutely clear that I can no longer disregard my body or treat it as something separate. A verse that I wrote a few years ago comes to mind:

The real truth is simply this:
my soul came into the world
to dwell in this fragile body.
I am the house that I inhabit.

I'd like to think that all these symptoms are what I'm told Japanese Buddhists call *sansoshima*: the obstacles that crop up along the path to significant change, which disappear once the change has occurred, but time will tell.

CHAPTER 13

CAPTAIN MIDNIGHT

Ted the Cockapoo appeared in our lives in March 2014. Chris loved dogs and her best-beloved Doogie had died in 2006. For some years she couldn't bear the thought of getting another dog and then our hard-working, frequent-travelling lifestyle made it impossible. When she fell ill, things changed: we rooted ourselves more firmly at Folly Cottage and worked much less. I managed to obtain permission from the management company of my flat in Lyme Regis to set aside its no pets rule, so the way was clear.

We got Ted (who is snoozing on the bench seat opposite me as I write) from a breeder in Burton-on-Trent. He sat on Chris's lap all the way home and has loved car travel ever since. "You know, I'm really glad that I made it possible for you to have a dog," I said to Chris a few months later.

"Sometimes, you are stupid beyond belief," she replied, laughing. "We got him for you."

It was only after she died, when Ted and I were alone in the house, that I really understood what she had meant. She had wanted me to have a companion to ease me through the grief of losing her. It was a stroke of genius: thinking of Ted's needs stops me disappearing into a morass of misery; walking him every day gets me out of the house. He comes to conferences with me and lies silently at my feet. His joy and loving energy are boundless. He sticks close by my side all day and sleeps next to me on the bed. Whenever my sorrow is sharpest and I weep, he jumps up to nuzzle my face; I hold him and sob until the storm subsides. He is endlessly loving, patient and uncomplaining. It's no exaggeration to say that I cannot imagine how I would have survived the past couple of years without him.

Last summer as Ted and I were coming to the end of our French sojourn, he discovered how to use the laptop for himself and has been blogging about life, love and dog biscuits ever since. Sometimes he can say things that I can't say and I'm grateful (though occasionally embarrassed) that he sees fit to tell the world how things are from his perspective. For reasons which he can best explain himself, his nom de plume is Captain Midnight. He has kindly agreed that I can include a few of his posts.

CAPTAIN MIDNIGHT
29 AUGUST 2015

Hello, Ted here.

Actually, Ted is an alias. I am really Captain Midnight, super-dog.

Finally, his back is turned. He's left the laptop turned on and now it's my turn to talk. He spends a long time deciding what to say and trying to be clever. I just write the plain truth.

"We'll go to France," he said. "The food is great."

He drinks a lot of red stuff from bottles and cooks bits of meat on the barbecue. His food is great. What do I get? Dog biscuits. French dog biscuits are just as appetising as British dog biscuits. I go on hunger strike sometimes until he puts a bit of meat or fish on them.

Then there's camping! Whose brilliant idea was that? As soon as I get the smells sorted out, spray a bit of urine and mark the territory, we're off somewhere else in the kennel (or camper van as he calls it). When we do get somewhere else I spend most of the day dossing around and barking at French people until he eventually decides he's tired of sitting on his backside "being a writer" and wants to go for a walk.

He usually finds somewhere nice for his walk, I'll give him that: some woods, a river, or a bit of seaside. I go with him to humour him and I always make a point of showing how "grateful" I am by pulling him along on the lead. He doesn't seem to like being on the lead much.

Last night he was moping around, feeling sorry for himself again. There was one of those full moon things and I had a brilliant idea! In the middle of the night, I clipped him to the lead and dragged him to the beach. There was no-one else there, just him and me. I thought he might like a good run around, so I unclipped him and waited. He just stood there.

I ran around like crazy, showing him what to do. I tried everything: I ate seaweed; ran into the sea; dug holes in the sand; and barked at the moon. It was huge fun. He still didn't catch on. Leader of the pack? I don't think so.

Then there's that other thing he does quite often. That thing when he makes a lot of noise and water comes out of his eyes. I jump up on his lap and lick his face when he does that. He puts his arms around me and makes even more noise. It usually doesn't last very long and I'm still trying to work out exactly what it means. He seems to like me being there when it happens.

He says it's because he feels lonely, so every night I let him share my bed in the kennel. I know they say that dogs should keep their humans at a distance, but I think that's a bit old fashioned. Fortunately, we only have to be "good enough" for our humans to develop self-confidence and a secure sense of attachment. My chap's coming on quite well, all things considered.

CAPTAIN MIDNIGHT'S CHRISTMAS LETTER
23 DECEMBER 2015

Well super-dog fans, it's been quite a year.

Obviously, the main thing is that it's the first one without The Missus. She went away 12 months ago but she hasn't gone completely. That will only happen when I can't smell her any more and I *can* still smell her, especially when Himself gets her clothes out of the wardrobe. Anyway, it makes Himself very sad and I have to leap into action to supply healing wags and slobbery kisses.

Nice people have invited us round for meals and parties this Christmas, but Himself has decided that we'll be hunkering down instead at Folly Cottage (which is lovely for walking in the woods, apart from the pheasant-murderers banging away) and then we'll be going to Lyme Regis for New Year so I can take him walking on Charmouth beach. People are more civilised down there...at least they don't take potshots at the seagulls.

There's a rumour of roast beef for Christmas dinner and the promise of a roaring log fire to follow, with the inevitable watching of old movies. I hope he doesn't make me sit through *Lassie* again.

I hate all that an-throp-o-morph-ism (big word for a small dog, I did have to ask Himself to spell it for me). You wouldn't catch me getting involved in anything like that, it's so demeaning.

We've had lots of visitors this year. Old friends from near and far including Australia, Canada, America and Scotland have called by to take Himself out for walkies (I go along of course) to cheer him up. His lady friends – the tall one and the short one who come round and make him laugh and make sure he has nice food to eat – have gone to South Africa (wherever that is, somewhere the other side of Dursley, I think). Apparently they'll be back, lithe and suntanned, in the spring. Himself seems a bit put out but good for them, I say. I wouldn't mind going; chasing a few springbok, that sort of thing. But, I digress.

Himself says that he's quite happy staying at home "being a writer" thank you very much. It took me a while to find out what he meant but I've now discovered what "being a writer" is. It's sitting at the kitchen table staring at a blank screen until his head bleeds. I give him lots of encouragement by snoozing on the bench right next to him. He says it helps but I can't really see how anyone's going to be interested in his stuff when they can read mine instead?

Another big thing this year was the five weeks we spent *en France* in the mobile kennel. It was pretty cosy, I can tell you. I managed to get a long rope so he felt less constricted on the lead but he's very slow so I had to drag him along. I watched a bit of *The Dog Whisperer* last night to get a few ideas but frankly I think he's untrainable.

I'm OK now but I have had a few medical mishaps this year: the tail incident and some accidental "self-harming" on my foreleg, to name but two. Any excuse to bang on the cone of shame! It's a bit undignified but I've got used to it. Speaking of undignified, he's just discovered "dog shampoo" and is experimenting on me regularly. I'm pretty sure he's in cahoots with those evil G.R.O.O.M.E.R.S.

Well that's probably enough for now. I only opened the laptop to wish you all a very merry Christmas and a happy and prosperous New Year.

DOGGEREL
10 MAY 2016

My human is a dog's best friend.
I treat him like a god,
Although of course I know he's just
An ordinary bod.

He calls me Ted or Teddifer
Or some invented name.
It matters not at all to me,
I love him just the same.

I love him when he's fast asleep
And when he's wide awake.
I sidle up and lick his chops,
I give my tail a shake.

Sometimes I take him to the beach
So he can throw a ball.
I have to run and fetch it, or
There'd be no ball at all.

He's not too bright at doggy stuff
And very hard to train;
I don't believe it when he says
He has a bigger brain.

Yes, there are times when I despair
That he will ever learn
To pee on lampposts as he should
With blissful unconcern.

On rainy days I lie around
While he sits down and writes;
I mostly nap and often dream
Of rabbits and of fights.

But when he's looking somewhere else
I pen a word or two.
Please keep it as our secret though!
He hasn't got a clue –

That Captain Midnight writes a blog
More popular by miles
Than all the stuff that he knocks out
In antiquated styles.

The thought of Teddy writing verse
Would give him quite a fright.
That's why I use a *nom de plume*
Every time I write.

He wouldn't understand I fear,
Why fate selected me
To challenge the immortal bard
And him to make the tea.

One Dog and His Man
24 June 2016

Himself is back from his American sojourn, gracing us with his presence for a few days before he buggers off again. Meanwhile, I spent the last three weeks with a very nice family the other side of Wotton-under-Edge. They looked after me very well indeed. Not "tasty toppers" on my biscuit but chicken. Simple enough you might think but apparently too difficult for my man to manage. I ask you!

That aside, it was nice to see Himself again. I gave him my very best greeting, which involves climbing up him like a tree until I am sitting on his head. He has no idea how I do it and frankly neither do I. It's a bit disconcerting all round but just another of my super-dog powers, I suppose.

He drove me back to Folly Cottage (I do like having a chauffeur) and I took him for a walk in the woods. As you know, I've struggled to train him to walk properly on the lead but I've got a new type of harness so he doesn't pull as much, which made the whole thing much more fun. He still threw the odd stick away, luckily I was there to fetch it back.

Later on, he made a cup of tea (never offered me any) and told me about his recent trip. It seemed mostly to be about putting

The Missus' ashes in the ground in various places. I can't quite understand why he did it unless he wants to go back later to dig them up and eat them, which does seem rather unlikely. But there's nowt as queer as folk, as I was saying to my Yorkshire terrier chums at the Kennel Club the other day.

Apparently, he's got a bit more travelling to do and then we're going camping in Ireland later in the summer in Plastic Rosie (our mobile kennel, or camper van as he calls it). It should be nice once we get across the watery bit. I've written a special note for him on the holiday shopping list:

DON'T FORGET THE CHICKEN

NOT MY FINEST HOUR
3 AUGUST 2016

Captain Midnight here, reporting from the mobile kennel (or the camper van as Himself calls it) on a farm somewhere in Ireland.

He did tell me the name of where we are but it slipped my mind after the riverbank debacle. You probably noticed that I'm still a bit wet, especially round the ears. Does anyone know why they take so long to dry? Beats me.

Why am I wet?

That was the riverbank thing.

Himself said that he was bored sitting down and writing all day.

"Let's go for a walk then," I suggested.

"Ooh yes," he said, jumping up on his hindlegs, all excited.

So I clipped him to the lead to stop him getting lost and took him down the path to the river for a stroll. For a treat, I decided to let him off once we were clear of the farm and he couldn't chase the livestock. Naturally, I went ahead to check for danger and interesting smells and came across the river. It looked rather inviting so I got into the water: a stylish leap followed by a bit of doggy paddle.

Getting in wasn't the problem, it was getting out again.

Somehow the bank was further up than it had been down. I didn't want to use my super-dog powers of levitation in broad daylight so I woofed until Himself clambered down the bank and hoicked me out by the collar. He made a fuss of me; asked if I was alright; gave me a cuddle; suggested that I didn't do it again; then walked on ahead as if he was the one in charge. All rather embarrassing.

Himself is only a pup and you're probably thinking that I shouldn't have let him off the lead. But how else is he going to learn?

CHAPTER 14

PARTING GIFTS

I began this book with an ending and I want to draw it to a close by going back in time to the last few days of Chris's life that preceded that ending. Anyone reading this who has been bereaved through chronic illness will know that anticipating the death of a loved one prefigures the grief that is to come. We feel the loss even before it has occurred but must contain it somehow for the sake of the one who is dying as we try to wring every last moment out of what time remains.

Perhaps we are physically caring for them as well, with all the strain that entails. In the midst of medical procedures and the comings and goings of friends, nurses and carers, it can be hard to sustain the one relationship that we most care about. If we are lucky, we get the chance to say goodbye before we are parted forever. This is the account of our parting, written a few weeks after Chris died on 3 December 2014.

~ ~ ~ ~

It's Friday night, 28 November 2014. Karen and Dick have gone back to their hotel after having supper with us. We're on our own now and getting ready for bed. Chris is sitting on the commode and we're talking about the day. She suddenly stops mid-sentence.

"What's the matter?" I ask.

"Seizure," she says.

The base of her neck, near her left clavicle, has started twitching. I lay my right palm flat on the spot to calm her. "Let's see if we can make it go away," I say. Sometimes, if we catch it early enough, that's all it takes: putting my hand on her can break the feedback loop and dissipate an impending fit. But not this time. The twitching amplifies under my hand and the fit starts to build. The muscles on the left side of her torso and in her left leg begin to spasm.

"Midazolam," I say. "I won't be a minute. Don't go anywhere." She tries to smile at my feeble joke but her eyes are widening with fear. I dash into the kitchen, grab our emergency kit and go back to her side. "Quick," she says.

"Easy-peasy," I say, inserting the nozzle of the plastic syringe through the rubber membrane of the medicine bottle. I pull the plunger and load the syringe with a dose of midazolam. She's shaking now, head rolling. I hold her steady and flush half the dose into the right side of her mouth. She grabs her face and massages the medicine into the highly absorbent tissue between her gums and cheek, as we've been taught by the epilepsy nurse. After a few seconds, we repeat the procedure on the left side.

Now comes the hardest part, we have to wait for the medication to take effect. There's always a lag of a few minutes before it works. But time goes out of kilter and it seems like an eternity. I put my arms around Chris and hold her. "It's alright," I say. "We know this stuff works. It will stop. We just have to be patient."

"That's good. Keep telling me," she says.

The words judder from her mouth. I know that the calmer she is, the sooner the fit will stop. "It's alright, baby. It's alright."

Eventually the convulsions subside and the fit is over. Based on past experience, two things are going to happen in the next few minutes: she'll pee (and possibly poo) uncontrollably and she'll pass out. She's still sitting on the commode, which is a mixed blessing. If she passes out before she can get back into bed, I'll have to call the paramedics to come and lift her because I can't do it on my own.

We're lucky. Things happen in the right order and ten minutes later she's clean and tidy and fast asleep in bed. I put her clothes away and sort out the commode. When everything is done, I sit on the edge of the bed and look at her. The fit had been a mild one and we'd caught it early.

I lean over and kiss her forehead. She doesn't stir. The midazolam has knocked her out. I go upstairs and fetch the camping mattress from the office, lay it on the floor at the end of her bed and stretch out under a duvet. I don't like being too far away when she's had a fit. I catch myself thinking that she probably won't wake up in time for the commode but I might get three or four undisturbed hours and that it's a price worth paying. I'm not proud of the thought but I fall asleep anyway.

Wendy from the agency arrives at 9.30 the next morning to get Chris up. I'd made her a mug of miso earlier and noticed that she was sluggish: she'd struggled to sit up and was slow to respond when I spoke to her. It happened sometimes after a fit. It might be a consequence of the seizure itself or the lingering effect of the midazolam. Wendy gives me a sideways look but I'm not unduly worried.

It's nearly 11.00am (half an hour longer than usual) by the time Chris is washed, dressed and sitting at the kitchen table. Ted and I have been to the woods for his morning walk and I make a late breakfast for Chris and me: yoghurt with raspberries and freshly milled sesame seeds, toast with butter and marmite that Chris spreads herself. I look at the diary.

"Busy day today, sweetheart. Karen and Dick are coming round, Richard's driving over to take me out to lunch and Carole said she'd pop in this afternoon."

There's a slight but perceptible lag before Chris speaks, as though she's chewing on my words to digest them before responding. "Are we going out for lunch tomorrow?"

"We could," I reply. "You, me, Dick and Karen. We could go to Abbey Home Farm."

"I like going there for lunch," she says. "I want to finish the Mort Brod. Is Nicola coming?"

I check the diary again. "She's coming on Monday afternoon to help you finish it, and we've got the first visit to the hospice on Friday." I know that she's looking forward to starting there. They've offered us 12 weekly visits and she is thrilled at the thought of committing to a process that assumes she will be alive in three months' time.

The day goes according to plan and I help Chris into bed at about 11.30pm. As I kiss her goodnight, she breaks off and says, "I'm scared of having another fit tonight. What if I can't reach the bell? What if you don't hear me?"

It's the first time she's said anything like this. We both know that the more stressed and worried she is, the more likely it is that she will actually have a seizure. "If you're really worried," I say, "we've got the clonazepam. The epilepsy nurse said that we can use it as a preventative. I can get you one of those if you like. They're just tablets."

"Yes, please."

I fetch the medicine box from the kitchen and read the instructions: "One tablet as required." I help Chris sit up, pass her a mug of water and offer the pill on my open palm. She picks it off and swallows it, then settles down for sleep. For the first time in months, she sleeps all night and so do I. Her sheets and duvet are soaking wet in the morning and I strip the bed while she's on the commode, find a fresh duvet, and change the linen. No agency women today: Liz is unwell and Wendy has a family commitment. We use wet wipes and a flannel to wash and I help Chris get dressed.

It's a slow business. When I speak, she squints at me with a look of intense concentration as if she's finding it hard to hear what I'm saying. "I'm tired," she says.

"Why don't you stay in bed for a bit then? That pill has made you woozy."

I bring her breakfast in bed and take Ted down the road for five minutes. I daren't leave her on her own any longer. She sleeps most of the morning but stirs when Karen and Dick arrive at midday. I can see that we're not going to get to Abbey Home Farm in time for lunch. "I'll cook for us," says Karen. "There's a load of food in the house." Chris loves Karen's cooking and she agrees to forgo the outing. She gets out of bed and sits at the kitchen table for a few hours, busying herself with the "eye-pokers" and chatting quietly. She's still dopey.

I go upstairs to the office and call the doctor. I eventually get through to the on-call doctor. He's not our regular GP and I have to explain the circumstances in detail. He's good though. "The clonazepam could still be active in her body. It's a powerful drug. If you give her any tonight, stick to half a tablet." He pauses. "It could just be her condition, you know. It sounds like you are doing everything you can. I'm very sorry. Don't hesitate to call me back. Any time at all. That's what I'm here for."

I thank him and hang up. By the time I come downstairs, Chris is back in bed. Dick sits with her while I take Ted out for a breather and Karen serves dinner. It's late by the time we eat, sitting around Chris's bed. She's sitting up, leaning against the backrest. Cushions prop her tray in place and she eats one-handed using the special fork that she got while she was in hospital. It's a convivial meal. Ted begs unsuccessfully for scraps as we fill our bellies with roast vegetables and leftover lamb.

Dick washes up and I dry the dishes. I can see that Chris and Karen are hugger-mugger in the next room but can't hear what they are saying. Karen and I have decided that tonight we're going to ask Chris to wear a pad to keep her dry. She hates the idea: "You can't wait to get me into those fucking things," was her last response to the idea but we're running out of bedding and it's often too late by the time she calls me, or perhaps by the time I've heard her call.

Karen and Dick take Ted out for his late-night walk while I sit with Chris. "They're going tomorrow," I say, hoping that naming what is hanging in the air will take some of the sting out of it. "I know they are going," Chris growls. "I'm not an idiot."

"It's been a good visit," I say.

Chris begins to weep. "I hate saying goodbye," she says. "I'll never see them again." I lean in and hold her hand. I can't think of anything to say that won't make things worse.

Karen and Dick come back. It's wet outside and Dick traipses mud into the house, smearing the already stained white rug beside Chris's bed. He's apologetic but it doesn't matter. Nothing matters really except that Chris is dying. I can see that we're moving towards the end game now. I don't know how long we've got but her physical condition and cognition have taken a dive in the past few days.

Karen and I help Chris change into a brushed cotton nightgown. "Will you wear a pad tonight, sweetie?" Karen asks.

Chris stiffens and says nothing.

"What's the problem?" Karen continues. "It'll be more comfortable for you. Less chance of bedsores."

"My dad," says Chris, crying. "My dad had to wear those things." Deep sobs wrack her body. "I couldn't help him," she blurts. "I was scared. I ran away."

"You were very young," I say. "You did your best and your mum was with him. He wasn't alone."

"I don't want to be alone."

"You aren't alone," I say. "You are surrounded by friends who love you. I love you and I'm not going anywhere. I'll be with you whatever happens. I promise."

"Karen's going."

"They have to go home. But they'll be back." I look at Karen.

"Christmas, maybe. Or New Year," says Karen.

The promise of another visit in a few weeks' time is a mirage but it offers hope and it's enough to shift the mood. Chris agrees to wear the pad and we put it on her. I give her half a tablet of clonazepam, lower the backrest and arrange the pillows. She grabs the bed stick and heaves herself onto her side.

"Goodnight, sweetie," Karen says. "See you tomorrow." She leaves with Dick to return to their hotel four miles away. "Call me if you need anything," she says to me as they go out the door. "We'll be fine," I say, realising as they drive away that I had been hoping that Karen would stay overnight.

The clonazepam has worked its tranquillising magic and Chris is drifting towards sleep as I go back into the house. I'm feeling guilty because I know that I gave it to her more for my benefit than for hers because I'm so tired. I go upstairs and crawl into the put-you-up with a guilty conscience but even that doesn't keep me awake for more than five minutes.

Liz comes at 10.00 the next morning. Reducing the clonazepam dose by half doesn't seem to have made any difference. Chris is moving in slow motion. It takes 90 minutes for her to get washed and dressed, sitting on the perching stool by the sink. Ted gets his morning walk and I sort out the daily medications before making our usual breakfast. Karen and Dick call in at noon on their way to the airport to say goodbye.

Chris is silent after they leave, her shoulders slumped. "Nicola's coming in an hour or so to help you finish the Mort Brod, and Sue H. is coming this afternoon to stay for a couple of days," I say, hoping that this will cheer her up.

"Good," she says. "Where are my eye-pokers?"

I put the bag of eyeliners and mascara brushes on the table and set down the mirror in front of her. "Fill your boots," I say. "I've got a couple of calls to make, OK?"

I go upstairs to the office and call the surgery. This time I get through to our GP, Rachel Hampson. I explain the palaver with the clonazepam over the weekend. "Don't give her any tonight," she says. "We'll see how she does. I'll get the district nurse to call in later to check her over but call me if you're worried."

Next, I call Tania, the Macmillan nurse at the hospice. "You must be exhausted," she says. "I'll get some night cover arranged. I should be able to find someone later this week. We only use trained nurses so she'll be in good hands." I feel tears of relief welling up. I'm running on empty and I don't think I can do many more nights on my own. "Thank you," I say. "I feel very proud to live in a country where we look after each other in this way. It's an extraordinary thing."

"You're welcome," she says. "Don't worry. We'll look after her... and you."

Nicola Clarke arrives just after 1.00pm and stays for an hour. She attaches the digital image of a skull that Chris has had printed to the reverse of the Mort Brod. It's a tricky process that uses a half-metre-wide roll of double-sided adhesive film. Then she sprays the whole thing with fixative to make it weather-proof and hangs it up to dry. "Are you pleased with it?" she asks Chris.

"It's just like I imagined," she replies. "Thank you. I couldn't have finished it without you."

"It's been a privilege to work on it," says Nicola.

I make some lunch and Nicola leaves for her choir practice. "It was good when we sang together with Carole, wasn't it?" I say.

"All those years I thought I couldn't sing," Chris says. "Crap."

"Yeah. Do you remember the 'Choir of the Damned' we did at the ISB Summer School? That was huge fun."

"And you did the storytelling with Jed…"

"He and Jo were brilliant at our wedding. I'll never forget them singing 'Sweetheart Come' as you walked on Robert's arm into the room at Matara." Less than a year has passed since we got married and I'm pleased to have invoked the memory of our wedding. "William and Juliet are coming over for our anniversary next week."

"I'm looking forward to that," she says.

I'm wondering if it will ever happen but I manage to keep a straight face.

Sue Hollingsworth arrives in the afternoon. I go out to help her bring her bags in from the car. "What time are you off to Lyme?" she asks.

"Chris is too ill, Sue. I can't go."

"Pity," she says. "You look knackered."

"I can't leave her. She's had a couple of fits recently."

"You know best. I can look after her at night, though. Give you a break."

"That would be marvellous. I can sleep out in the Shepherd Hut. You can come and get me if anything happens."

"I'll be fine with her, Geoff. But if it makes you feel better, I promise that I'll come and get you."

Sue hands me her suitcase and follows me into Folly Cottage. She goes over and hugs Chris who looks back at her with big round eyes, emphasised by mascara and eyeliner. "Wow! You look great," Sue says. "Love the makeup."

Chris looks slightly embarrassed. "Thought I'd give it a go," she says. "Never too late."

I leave the two of them together and go back up to the office for a while. It's a chance to breathe out and there's still stuff from the accountant and the insurance company to sort out. Sue cared for her husband Jim when he was dying from a heart condition a few years ago. She's rock solid. "Thank God she's here," I say to myself.

We eat early that evening at the kitchen table. Chris seems to have more energy than earlier in the day. Perhaps the clonazepam is finally wearing off, I think. There's some stock left over from Karen's cooking. Sue adds some cooked vegetables and whizzes them into a dense, creamy soup. Between the three bowls, she puts a dish with the chopped-up remains of the roast lamb we had on Thursday for Thanksgiving to add to the soup. Chris reaches across with her good hand, picks up the dish and tips the entire contents into her soup. Then she ladles the soup into her mouth in a kind of feeding frenzy, splashing it onto her dress. I say nothing and mop it up with some kitchen roll. Sue removes the bowls and serves the venison pies she's brought, with gravy and broccoli. Chris demolishes her plateful before we are halfway through ours. I've never seen her eat with such ferocity. Afterwards there is Key lime pie and cream which disappears just as quickly. Sue looks sideways at me and raises an eyebrow. I shrug in reply. I have no idea what is going on.

After supper, I brief Sue on the emergency procedure and show her how to use the midazolam if Chris has a fit. Between us, we help Chris get ready for bed, negotiate the commode and tuck her up for the night. I retire to the Shepherd Hut with Ted and a lantern. I can see the lights in Folly Cottage being turned out one by one as Sue clears up and goes to bed. I blow out the lantern and close my eyes, imagining that it won't be long before there's a knock on the door.

But it's morning when I wake up. Sue is loading sheets into the washing machine in the kitchen when I go in the house to use the loo. "How was it?" I ask.

"Up seven or eight times," Sue says. "I made a joke of it – like I was the genie of the lamp – when she rang the bell."

"My sense of humour seems to vanish at night," I say.

"It wasn't all sweetness and light. She got angry with me too."

"It's so hard to see her struggling," I say.

"She said last night, 'This is not alright, is it, Sue?' I think she's had just about enough," says Sue.

I look through the doorway into the bedroom. Chris is still sleeping. I dole out her morning medication into a shot glass, put yoghurt and fruit into bowls for breakfast and take Ted down the road for a quick trot.

When I get back, Chris is awake but drowsy. She's had a couple of mouthfuls of yoghurt and the pills have vanished. I kiss her and give her a hug. "Tired today?"

She nods.

"Rest awhile," I say. "Wendy will be here soon to get you up."

She sinks back onto the pillow and closes her eyes.

Wendy arrives at 10.15am with Kate, a second carer. They go into the bedroom. I stay in the kitchen and leave them to it.

"How did you and Ted sleep in the hut?" asks Sue.

"I must have got about six hours," I say. "It was a godsend, thank you."

We chat for a while until Wendy comes in to see us. "We couldn't get her up," she says.

"What happened?" I ask.

"We got her washed and dressed on the edge of the bed but she couldn't stand up for the walker. She got into the wheelchair but she kept slumping over. She's back in bed."

"How did you manage that?" I ask.

"We pulled her upright between us and turned her around until she could drop onto the bed. I don't think she'll be getting up today. It was the best we could do. I'm sorry." Wendy fills out the daily report form and leaves with Kate in tow.

I go into the bedroom to see Chris. She's wearing her favourite linen dress and lying on her right side, leaning on the backrest. "How are you, sweetheart?"

"Headache," she says. "Bonce hurts."

I fetch a paracetamol, put my arm around her to prop her up and offer her the pill and a glass of water. She squints at me as if puzzled. "For your hurty bonce," I say.

"Hurty bonce," she repeats and opens her mouth to drink. As she does so, soggy white fragments spill out. I realise that she must have pouched the pills she was supposed to take an hour ago. I hold the glass to her lips and tip so she can drink.

"Swallow," I say.

She gulps the water. "Open wide." She opens her mouth like an obedient child at the dentist. The pills have gone. She takes the paracetamol from my palm and finds her mouth. Her hand is shaking. I tip the glass again and she swallows. "Show me," I say. She opens her mouth again. It's empty. "Well done."

"Fucking pills," she mumbles and then laughs. "Fucking pills."

"Rest awhile," I say. "Give the paracetamol a chance to work."

She closes her eyes and sinks into the pillow. I sit beside her for a while until she dozes off. Sue comes in. "Why don't you take Ted down to the woods for a proper walk?" she says. "You could both do with getting out. I'll stay here."

I don boots, jacket, gloves and scarf then clip Ted's lead to his collar and set off for Kingscote Woods. I take my mobile phone ("just in case") but it's not needed. I let Ted off his lead and we take the upper path through the woods. The ferns are dripping wet, the tracks are muddy and Ted wallows and snuffles in every puddle he can find. A pheasant claps its wings and heaves itself into the air a few yards away. Ted chases after it, woofing indignantly, until it is beyond reach. He trots back to me, delighted with his exploit, tail held high as if to say, "Did you see what I did?" I give him a morsel of dried liver, from a bag in my pocket, for being so clever and we go on our way, looping down onto the lower path at the end of the wood for the return journey. Back at Folly Cottage, I hose Ted off in the back garden, rinse my boots and go inside.

"She's calling for you," says Sue. "Started just now."

I go straight into the bedroom. Chris is still on her right side. Her eyes are closed but she's speaking. "Geoff," she says. "Help me over, Geoff." I reach down and help her roll towards the other side of the bed. I grab her shoulder and hold her in position as I lift the backrest out and replace the pillows. I'm worried about trapping her left arm under her body if she goes too far onto her left side. Her right arm flails across the bed as if reaching for the bed stick on the far side. "Help me over, Geoff. Help me over." Her voice is insistent, unvarying. I've not seen nor heard her like this before. I suddenly wonder if she's asking me to do more than help her move across the bed. I ease her onto her left side then lie down beside her with my arm round her shoulders. "That's the best I can do, sweetheart," I say.

She stops struggling and I feel her body relax against mine. She hasn't opened her eyes and I sense that she is drifting towards unconsciousness. What if she doesn't wake up? There isn't much time.

I lean my head close to hers and speak into her ear: "Do you remember the story I wrote for you about Numitorum the Great Bear?"

"Yes," she says and a smile crosses her face.

"How when it's time for bears and half-and-halfers to go home, Numitorum gives them a hundred-year hug and then sends them off to play among the stars?" Tears well up in my eyes and I fight back a sob. "That's where you are going, my lovely girl." I let the image sink in. Chris says nothing but I know she's heard me.

"I love you, darling woman," I say. "I love you with all of my heart."

There's a pause.

"Thank you," she murmurs. "Thank you."

Her voice trails off and very soon she is sleeping in my arms.

Somehow I know that she is never going to wake up.

Unless you had known her very well, you would not have been able to guess that – despite her extraordinary gift for friendship – Chris found it hard to believe that she herself was worthy of love. Often I found loving her the easiest and most natural thing in the world; but when the shadow of self-doubt ruled her heart, it was neither.

For me, our last weeks together were wonderful when she let me in and excruciating when (sometimes because of my anxiety or clumsiness, and sometimes for reasons I didn't understand) she pushed me away. As her final hours approached, my greatest fear was that she would die without knowing – really knowing – that I loved her. But at the last moment, her simple *thank you* was the clearest possible message that she accepted my love.

Perhaps this is the greatest gift of all: not just to love but to take the greater risk of allowing oneself to be loved. As with so many other things, Chris taught me what really matters in the end.

Push me over, you say aloud
as you twist and turn in bed.
Help me Geoff. Push me over.
Again and again you ask me.

I can only move you slightly
but it seems to be enough.
You settle into the pillow,
eyes closed as if for sleep.

So, I lie down by your side
and breathe into your ear:
*Do you remember the story,
the one I wrote just for you?*

(I want you to see the image
of that great bear in heaven
hugging you for 100 years)
You smile and whisper, *Yes.*

I hold you closer so I can say
the only thing that matters:
I love you my darling woman,
I love you with all my heart.

You haven't breath for much;
you are getting ready to leave.
Thank you, you say, *thank you*,
and slip away into the silence.

LIFE BELONGS TO THE LIVING

In the opening chapter, "Here Be Dragons," I wrote that I would to try to show something of my journey through the *terra incognita* of loss and bereavement. I have kept close to the messy reality of lived experience by drawing heavily on what I wrote at the time rather than present a well-ordered history or suggest that there are universal lessons to be learned from my story. I see myself not as an expert guide but as a fellow-traveller doing my best to make sense of things that most of us will experience at some time in our lives, and I hope that my personal search for solace offers you something of value.

Bereavement does not end but this book must. It's two years since Chris died; grief continues to catch me unawares but the anguish of loss is no longer ever-present. Out of the blue, a new love has opened my heart once again. A new phase of life has begun, one which might equally be worth writing about but which seems to herald the beginning of a different story. It feels important to acknowledge the shift and appropriate to do so as an epilogue.

Suddenly, I have a future to dream into as well a past to mourn. What was stirring in me a year ago, as I attended the constellation workshop described in the chapter "Being and Becoming," is manifesting in my life as a passionate, loving relationship within which there is also room for Chris's memory.

At first, I hesitated to tell anyone about my new relationship. After what the constellation had revealed, I was quite sure that Chris would be smiling down on us, but I was anxious that Chris's family and friends might think that it was too soon. Actually, when

I did tell them, they were universally approving and warm-hearted in their responses. My doubts had been unworthy of their generous natures.

Nevertheless, I was circumspect in how I wrote about the burgeoning relationship in my blog posts. I did not want to deceive readers by pretending it wasn't happening, but neither did I want to jinx the relationship by making it public knowledge too soon. I alluded to the possibility in a post I wrote when I returned briefly to New York, immediately after our first date.

New York, New York
3 July 2016

It's the best part of 50 years since I first came here as a student in the 1960s and I've been back many times. Chris and I came quite often to stay with our friends Dick and Karen, and two days ago I was a guest at their wedding. It's been a long time coming (they've been together for 20 years) and maybe our own wedding and Chris's illness and death gave them a nudge.

Yesterday, I visited the 9/11 Memorial Plaza. It's said that we don't do grief well in Western society, but this memorial is stunning in its simplicity and profundity. Within the footprints of the Twin Towers, two massive acre-square waterfalls cascade in thousands of slender streams, combining to form sheets of water that are gathered and held briefly in pools 30 feet below, before plunging deep into the earth. At the perimeter, the names of all the known victims are etched into bronze tablets.

It was on the day after 9/11 that Chris and I, who had been friends for some time, reached out to each other and became more than friends, so although we didn't lose anyone we knew, the event had some personal significance for us. I went back this morning clutching a single stem of gerbera, which I offered in memory of those who died in the attack and of the time Chris and I were together in the years that followed.

Then I caught the subway to Penn Station and walked along 34th Street to the Empire State Building. I wanted to do something that Chris and I had not done together in New York, to symbolise the arrival of new energy and new love in my life. It took an hour to get up to the observation deck on the 86th floor, but the view of the city and the sense of limitless possibility it exudes made the queuing and cramped lifts worthwhile.

As I looked downtown at the gleaming One World Trade Centre, I recalled that, out of the smouldering rubble of the Twin Towers, workers rescued a badly damaged Callery pear tree. With loving care, it has thrived, been replanted in the plaza, and christened the Survivor Tree. It stands as a modest reminder of the universal impulse for life in the aftermath of death.

So, I'm flying home this evening in good spirits, with love and gratitude for all that Chris gave me, and with high hopes for what the future might hold.

ॐ ॐ ॐ ॐ

Over the next few weeks, as my new love and I spent more time together, it became clear that we both wanted this to be a lasting relationship. It was time for the world to know about us, and who better than Ted (aka Captain Midnight) to spread the word? He pounced on the keyboard when I wasn't looking and posted the following on my blog.

Now We Are Three
2 August 2016

Captain Midnight here with good news.

Her name is Hedda. Himself is smiling a lot more since she turned up. I say turned up, but it was all my doing really.

I know it's my job to keep an eye on him, but a few weeks ago I got to thinking that it would be nice to share the load. So, I took him down the hill in Lyme Regis to visit old friends, and when I spotted Herself, sitting in their garden, bathed in sunlight, I pounced.

Himself was drinking tea, completely oblivious. Duh!

I tugged at the lead to get his attention and looked pointedly in her direction. He still didn't get it, so I woofed and dragged him across the lawn to say hello. You'd think he'd know what to say, being a writer and all, wouldn't you? But no. He hemmed and hawed, mumbled, went red and sat down.

Hopeless.

She seemed friendly enough but he clearly needed help. Summoning my super-dog powers, I jumped onto his lap and looked winsome. It's one of my most appealing looks, well-nigh irresistible.

"Nice dog," she said. "Yours?"

"His name is Ted," said Himself.

"Suits him," she said. "My name's Hedda."

"Mine's Geoff," he said. "Hello, Hedda."

The ice was broken and my work was done. They haven't stopped talking since. He tells me they've been out to dinner, and to the circus (I wasn't invited to either, which is a bit rich). But I did go to visit Hedda at her house and, last weekend, she came to stay with us in Lyme. She gave me chicken and we all paddled in the sea, which I enjoyed very much.

Himself told me they want to see a lot more of each other. I said that three is better than two and that she is very welcome to join our pack. "Absolutely," he said blithely, as if it had been his idea in the first place.

Of course dear reader, we know what it really was.

A triumph for Captain Midnight.

Babe magnet.

༈ ༈ ༈ ༈

Writing in the persona of Captain Midnight made it easier to speak openly for the first time about being with Hedda. After all, it wasn't really me talking, was it? The truth was that I wasn't yet ready to confess the depth of my feelings in such a public way. But, after we spent what would have been Chris's birthday together, I knew it was time to speak about Hedda in my own voice.

THE BEAR NECESSITIES
22 AUGUST 2016

Captain Midnight, Hedda and I are in Crickhowell, Powys for a few days. Yesterday would have been Chris's 50th birthday so we went to The Bear (very appropriately named, we thought) for a gin and tonic to mark the occasion. At 7.00pm we raised our glasses to join friends around the world in a virtual toast to her memory and to wish her a Happy Birthday.

Hedda asked me to tell her more about Chris. For nearly an hour, she listened as I spoke about Chris's life and work; her art-making and clowning; her intellectual prowess and inspired teaching. I spoke about her illness and her death; her courage and creativity; her enthusiasm for life; and her gift for friendship.

We talked about our experiences of love and loss and finding love again. Then we moved from the sofa and took our table for dinner with Ted at our feet, turned our gaze towards each other, and began to make plans for the days ahead. I bathed in the warmth of Hedda's brilliant smile as we spoke, and I felt my heart expand.

It was a pivotal moment, in which – so to speak – my centre of gravity shifted from the past to the present, and to the possibility of creating a shared future with this wonderful woman. I was ready to love again.

As Goethe said: "Life belongs to the living."

≈ ≈ ≈ ≈

Although I had often talked with Hedda about Chris, this was the first time that she had joined me in actively remembering and celebrating Chris's life. I realised at the time how significant it was for us to honour Chris together and how equally important it was afterwards for us to turn towards life and each other.

After Crickhowell, Hedda and I went to Shetland for a week. When she wasn't working at the Film Festival, which was the reason for our visit, we hung out and got to know each other better. We watched seals and sea otters; walked hand in hand along pristine beaches; photographed spectacular cliffs; visited an architect turned silversmith; had many cups of tea and cake; found a couple of good selkie tales; and bought locally made jumpers at half the price we would have paid in London.

Meeting Hedda has been an extraordinary and unexpected delight: she has brought love, beauty and joy back into my life. To fall in love again after losing Chris is a constant source of wonder. That it should happen to me at the age when my grandfather would cycle to the post office to collect his pension only doubles my amazement.

I am struggling to find a language to explain how this happened. But love is a mystery, perhaps the deepest mystery of all, and the mundane lexicon of our workaday lives is quite inadequate to describe the workings of the heart. As I wrote to Hedda, in response to the sentiment expressed by a lovingly made gift:

> The heart speaks, not in syllables
> but in the songs of jewelled birds
> and the lightness of a feather.
> Love gives us wings, not words.

ABOUT THE AUTHOR

Geoff Mead was the first member of his family to go to university (and the first to drop out). He quickly returned to complete his studies in mediaeval history after a salutary period washing cars for a living. With not much idea of what he really wanted to do, he cut off his shoulder-length hair and joined the police service which he left three decades later in his fifties as a chief superintendent.

Soon afterward, Geoff discovered the magic of stories and began to explore their power to liberate the human spirit. With a decade of his late wife Chris Seeley's encouragement behind him, he now enjoys the life of a writer, performing storyteller, freelance academic, and leadership consultant.

Geoff and Chris met in 2001 at University of Bath as he was finishing his PhD and she was beginning hers. They lived together for the next dozen years, enjoying and supporting each other's creative work in the world and got married in December 2013, a few months after Chris had been diagnosed with an inoperable brain tumour. She died in December 2014 and he sought solace in writing the stories, reflections, and poems that eventually became this book.

Geoff's first book, *Coming Home to Story: Storytelling After Happily Ever After*, was published by Vala in 2011. His second, *Telling the Story: The Heart and Soul of Successful Leadership*, was published by Wiley/Jossey Bass in May 2104. He has a volume of poetry in print, *Zoëtrope*, published by Chrysalis, also in 2104. His first children's story, *Bear Child*, is due for publication by Floris Books in 2018.

Geoff has four grown-up children from an earlier marriage, five grandchildren, a beloved and incorrigible Cockapoo named Ted, and an entirely unreasonable love of Morgan sports cars. When not travelling, he divides his time between his late wife's house in the Cotswolds, and a flat in Lyme Regis where he dreams and writes in sight of the sea. Beyond all expectation, he now shares his life with a new love, Hedda, who took the picture above, whilst they were on holiday in Shetland.

ACKNOWLEDGEMENTS

This book is about the experience of bereavement following the death of my wife Chris Seeley in 2014. It is not a book I ever wanted to have reason to write. That I turned to writing for solace is a measure of her inspiration and encouragement for me to become a writer. Her love and creative energy have been my constant companions on every step of the journey from the first day we met until today, as I write these words of gratitude. Thank you Chris, for everything.

My grown-up children – Nicky, Jamie, Georgie, and Tom – have been amazingly supportive as I mourned the loss of someone of whom they were fond but was not their mother. I am so proud of you.

Nothing I can say here would be sufficient to thank Hedda Archbold for her love and generosity of spirit. She has welcomed me into her life in such a way that there has always been room for Chris's memory as our own relationship has blossomed. This book could only have been written with her open-hearted and unselfish support. When Chris died, I didn't think I would ever love again. I was wrong and I am blessed.

Old friends and new have sustained me through the most difficult of times, with both practical and moral support. Sue Hollingsworth and Peter Neall cocooned me in their loving arms for the first few days after Chris died, when I was incapable of doing anything more than making a cup of tea. They, Karen Karp, Kathy Skerritt, Carole Bond, Richard Olivier, and many others have consistently reached out to make sure that I was not drowning in sorrow. Some also offered hospitality and shared in my peregrination to far-flung places with Chris's ashes. You are too many to name here but you know who you are and you define the true meaning of friendship.

I owe special thanks to Judith Hemming of Moving Constellations, a dear friend whose counsel and therapeutic help I have valued for many years, for facilitating the constellation in Chapter 9, "Being and Becoming." She has been my soul-guide at so many critical junctures of my life, acting always with immaculate skill, wise judgement, and a compassionate heart.

Sincere thanks are also due to those who have directly contributed to bringing this book into the world: Alicia Carey, Principal of Hawkwood College who invited me to take up an Artist's Residency to kick-start the book; Sarah Bird, editor extraordinaire who gave invaluable feedback on an early draft of the manuscript; poet Jay Ramsay who helped me avoid too many solecisms in my poems; and friends William Ayot, Carole Bond, Paul MacDonald, Robert and Angel McNeer who generously allowed me to include their wise words and wonderful images in the text. I'm also grateful to all the readers of my blog www.cominghometostory.com and especially those who read my posts on bereavement and encouraged me to believe that it would be helpful to write a book telling the story more fully.

Jessica Kingsley and the staff at JKP have championed this book since its inception. They have striven with remarkable speed and efficiency to produce a book that is both easy on the eye and good to hold in the hand and I'm grateful for their tireless efforts to get it onto bookshelves in the form that I envisaged.

Finally, this is also where I get to acknowledge the extraordinary bundle of unconditional love that is my dog Ted (also known as Captain Midnight). He has slept by my side, licked my tears as I wept through waves of grief, bounced with joy at the prospect of every new day, and taught me how to live and laugh again. He is lying at my feet as I write these words, patiently waiting for me to finish so we can go to the beach.

Come on, boy.

Walkies!